WELCOME

Private Cole: "Why does it have to be us? Why us?"

Colour Sergeant Bourne: "Because we're here, lad. Nobody else. Just us."

For many people, the Anglo-Zulu War of 1879 is known only from the thrilling 1964 adventure film, *Zulu*. The origins of the conflict, the key players, and the battles that followed are largely forgotten by the public.

The pre-eminence of the Battle of Rorke's Drift in the public imagination is partly by design. The war was fought as little more than an imperialist land-grab that cost thousands of lives and made no meaningful strides towards its architects' aim, which was the creation of a single nation of South Africa.

In the wake of the chaos and cowardice of the Battle of Isandlwana, which in a single afternoon turned Zululand's overconfident invaders into a panicked force, fighting a retreat behind their own borders, the war's commander needed heroes to bolster his tainted reputation, and to rally the public and Parliament around the war.

This image is what endures: a row of rough and ready everymen in red coats holding firm against impossible odds. Like the sun helmets themselves, a brilliant dazzling white in the movie, but in reality, stained with tea to dull their lustre with dirty brown lest they draw in a spear or bullet, the story is a lot more complex. As you'll discover in this special bookazine, the Anglo-Zulu War had plenty of heroes,

a few villains, and a lot of men who fit somewhere between the two.

In an era of distrust in government, the memories of unpopular foreign wars and regime changes, and, conversely, a retreat into the imagined glories of the past, it's more important than ever to take a balanced view of Britain's colonial conflicts. Here, we celebrate the valour of the fighting men and the ingenuity of their leaders, hold to account the misguided ambitions, deceptions, cruelty and cowardice of those who let them down and remember the terrible loss of life to both sides in these unnecessary battles.

James Hoare
Editor

Black irregulars and Mounted Infantry from Fort Eshowe burn the kraal belonging to the Zulu King's brother, Dabulamanzi kaMpande.

CONTENTS

ABOVE RIGHT · *A patrol of 17th Lancers (Duke of Cambridge's Own) inspect their long-dead comrades in the shadow of the infamous Isandlwana Hill.*

ZULU

ISBN 978 1 80282 226 7
Editor: James Hoare
Senior editor, specials: Roger Mortimer
Email: roger.mortimer@keypublishing.com
Design: Mike Carr
Cover design: Dan Hilliard
Advertising Sales Manager: Brodie Baxter
Email: brodie.baxter@keypublishing.com
Tel: 01780 755131
Advertising Production: Debi McGowan
Email: debi.mcgowan@keypublishing.com

SUBSCRIPTION/MAIL ORDER
Key Publishing Ltd, PO Box 300, Stamford, Lincs, PE9 1NA
Tel: 01780 480404 **Fax:** 01780 757812
Subscriptions email: subs@keypublishing.com
Mail Order email: orders@keypublishing.com

Website: www.keypublishing.com/shop

PUBLISHING
Group CEO: Adrian Cox
Publisher: Jonathan Jackson
Head of Publishing: Finbarr O'Reilly
Head of Marketing: Shaun Binnington
Key Publishing Ltd, PO Box 100, Stamford, Lincs, PE9 1XP
Tel: 01780 755131 Website: www.keypublishing.com

PRINTING
Precision Colour Printing Ltd, Haldane,
Halesfield 1, Telford, Shropshire. TF7 4QQ

DISTRIBUTION
Seymour Distribution Ltd, 2 Poultry Avenue, London, EC1A 9PU
Enquiries Line: 02074 294000.

CHRISTIANITY, CIVILISATION AND COMMERCE

The British Empire in Africa, 1672 - 1878

"TAKE UP THE WHITE MAN'S BURDEN —
SEND FORTH THE BEST YE BREED —
GO BIND YOUR SONS TO EXILE
TO SERVE YOUR CAPTIVES' NEED;
TO WAIT IN HEAVY HARNESS,
ON FLUTTERED FOLK AND WILD —
YOUR NEW-CAUGHT, SULLEN PEOPLES,
HALF-DEVIL AND HALF-CHILD."
- RUDYARD KIPLING, THE WHITE MAN'S BURDEN (1899)

To men like Kipling, the great poet of the Raj, Britain's place in the world was one of immense responsibility. He wasn't numb to the darker sides of imperialism - if you look past some of his uncomfortable language, his writing is filled with criticism - but his faith that British rule made the world a better place endured.

To the late Victorians, empire was a civilising mission. An awesome responsibility to take 'backwards' and 'barbaric' indigenous people and raise them up through settlers, steam trains, Christianity and commerce, and displace what Kipling called "the tawdry rule of kings" with the firm, paternal hand of white administration.

This view had emerged in the mid-19th century from the minds of the liberal imperialists, inspired by the evangelical revival that drove the opposition to the slave trade and set against the great strides of the Industrial Revolution.

It did, of course, ignore the cultures and civilisations that already existed in Africa, which didn't comfortably fit European expectations of what this should look like. Instead, the imperialist saw a "half-devil" of cruel chieftains, superstitious witch doctors, cannibalism and tribal warfare, and a simple-minded "half-child"

who lived in a hut, wore animal skins and could be taught English, given a Bible, and put to work.

THE TAWDRY RULE OF KINGS

The Kingdom of England had come late to imperialism by European standards. Awed by the riches they had looted from returning Spanish ships in the Atlantic, starting in 1607 England made haste to catch up, settling on the eastern seaboard of North America.

Until the late 19th century, the only African resources that captivated Europe's great maritime powers was its indigenous population. Slave labour made the far-flung colonies in America and the Caribbean profitable, and by 1540 an estimated 10,000 Africans a year were being transported across the Atlantic in chains from West Africa.

Britain formally entered this gruesome market in 1672 when King Charles II gave the Royal African Company a 1,000-year monopoly on the supply of slaves to British sugar and tobacco plantations. The company was intrinsically linked to the crown by more than name. Its governor was James, Duke of York, the brother of the king who would go on to rule as James II. In his honour many slaves were branded "DY" on their chests.

The Royal African Company built forts (or factories) along the Slave Coast and Gold Coast from the Gulf of Guinea to the Bight of Benin, including what is now Ghana, Togo, Benin, and Nigeria. Headquartered in Cape Coast Castle, these forts held their human cargo which was bought by merchants from tribal leaders in the interior. A rhyme first recorded in 1849 but purporting to be much older went: "Beware, beware the Bight of Benin, for few come out though many go in."

One of their most prominent local partners was the powerful Kingdom of Ashanti, encompassing part of what is modern Ghana. The Ashanti initially caught the imagination of Portuguese traders in the 15th century thanks to their plentiful access to gold and the mildly narcotic kola nut - a source of caffeine that gives us the word 'cola'. The Ashanti had traditionally enslaved their defeated rivals and were only too happy to share the bounty. Growing rich on the trade of slaves, gold and kola, the Ashanti (Asante in Twi, a dialect of Akan, which means "because of war") expanded rapidly to conquer their neighbours, leading to more slaves, more wealth, and then more conquest.

The RAC's monopoly was whisked away in 1698 with the end of the Stuart dynasty and other companies sprung up, paying a service charge to access the RAC's network of forts. Gold, spices, ivory and palm oil were also traded, but these alone weren't enough to encourage any serious investment. Britain, France, Denmark, the Netherlands, and Portugal clung to the coastline of the west and southeast. The north and east of African were subject to exploitation by Muslim powers that long pre-dated European activity and the slave route through Zanzibar to the Arabian Peninsula lasted until 1900.

Approximately 12 million Africans were transported across the Atlantic between the 16th and 19th century, and an estimated 1.5 million died in the

ABOVE · *Queen Victoria Giving the Bible to an African Chief (The Secret of England's Greatness) by Thomas Jones Barker, 1861.*

ABOVE LEFT · *An 1880 illustration of Africans being driven to the coast by a rival tribe where they will be sold as slaves.* WELLCOME COLLECTION

crossing. Another four million dead are often overlooked because they died at the hands of slavers during capture or during their forced march to the coast.

Across the closing decades of the 18th century, the mood of the British public turned firmly against the inhuman slave trade, spurred on by Protestant evangelicals such as the Quakers, Methodists and Baptists. After years of rhetorical fisticuffs between the abolitionists and the plantation owners, Great Britain outlawed the trade in 1807, and ended the use of slave labour in the British Empire in 1833.

The bankrupt RAC had become the African Company of Merchants in 1752. Their role was ostensibly the management of trade in West Africa, but the trade in humans was a core component of that. They limped on following abolition until 1821 when they finally disbanded for having done too little to end the slave trade that they had grown rich on. Their forts and the surrounding lands they had accrued now came under a single governor appointed by the British government.

THE LIBERATED AND THE CONDEMNED

Between 1808 and 1860, the Royal Navy's West Africa Squadron patrolled the coast. Some 1,600 slave ships were captured, and 150,000 Africans freed by this humanitarian mission. It was a striking reversal of the British position, but one that allowed empire to endure and grow.

As early as 1787 the British had settled freed slaves in Freetown, Sierra Leone. However, it was really with the start of West Africa Squadron's mission in 1808, that Sierra Leone was established as a colony. The first migrants were former slaves who had fought with the British in the American Revolutionary War (1775–1783). They were being 'returned' to a country they had never seen and whose languages they didn't speak, and these English-speaking African-Americans were joined by Africans recently liberated by the Royal Navy.

Those freed from the slave ships could be 'sold' to British colonists as 'apprentices' for a 14-year stretch. Many were unpaid, subject to beatings by their 'employers', and if they tried to escape, they were returned to their workplace for punishment. It wasn't slavery, but at its worst, it was uncomfortably similar.

The men and boys were also offered up for the black levies of the Royal African Corps, a garrison force founded in 1804 for the protection of Britain's African holdings. Perversely, the lives of

ABOVE · *Hodge kneels on the right in* The Capture of Tubabecelong, Gambia *by Louis Desanges.*
PENLEE HOUSE GALLERY & MUSEUM

From Tortola in the British Virgin Islands, the 26-year old Private Samuel Hodge was part of the 4th West India Regiment sent to confront the rebellious warlord, Amar Faal, on the northern bank of the River Gambia.

After failing to break into Faal's stockade with rockets, Lieutenant Colonel George Abbas Kooli D'Arcy called for volunteers to hack at it by hand. Hodge grabbed an axe and joined the charge, but the fire was so fierce that the two officers were killed almost immediately (white officers in a black regiment make tempting targets) and most of the men wounded.

By the time he reached the stockade only D'Arcy, Hodge and another soldier, Private Boswell, were still on their feet. Hacking a hole large enough for a single man, Boswell was shot and killed, D'Arcy darted through the hole, followed by Hodge who hacked at the fastenings at the gate before he was wounded. The gates swung open and 4th West India Regiment poured in.

Hodge was promoted to lance-corporal and was presented the Victoria Cross on June 24, 1867. He never recovered from his wounds and died of fever in Belize in January 1868. He is the second black person to be awarded the Victoria Cross and the first black soldier (the first, William Hall, served with the Royal Navy).

ABOVE · *A 1727 study of Dutch and English slave forts facing each other at Accra, Gold Coast (now Ghana), along with the local curiosities.* WELLCOME COLLECTION

IMPERIAL FEDERATION.—MAP OF THE WORLD SHOWING THE EXTENT OF THE **BRITISH EMPIRE** IN 1886. STATISTICAL INFORMATION FURNISHED BY CAPTAIN J.C.R.COLOMB.M.P.FORMERLY R.M.A. BRITISH TERRITORIES COLOURED RED

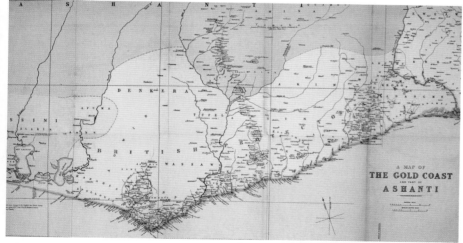

A MAP OF
THE GOLD COAST
AND PART OF
ASHANTI

ABOVE · *A map of the British Empire in 1888, just before the 'Scramble for Africa'. The only parts of the continent under British rule are Cape Colony and British West Africa.*

LEFT · *The Gold Coast in 1874, with the powerful Ashanti Kingdom to the north.*

those freed from unjust imprisonment were in the hands of men who had been condemned. In the 18th century, penal brigades of army criminals were sent to garrison the slave forts, and this tradition lived on. Deserters were taken from the prison hulks that sat filthy and overcrowded in the Thames and dispatched to West Africa. If General Sir Arthur Wellesley thought the British soldier in 1813 was "the scum of the Earth", his thoughts on the Royal African Corps would have turned the air blue.

This posting was as good as the death sentence and in an 1828 sample of 796 soldiers there were 986 cases of malaria, blackwater fever or dysentery, and of that number 377 (nearly half) died. Fortunately for both the men being punished and the civilian population, the Royal African Corps were disbanded by the 1840s and the protection of West Africa became the responsibility of local militias and West India Regiments, who were judged more capable of enduring heat and humidity.

Even before Africa became a part of their tour of duty, the issues of manpower following the end of slavery led the West India Regiments to establish a depot in Sierra Leone in 1812 for the training of African recruits for service in the Caribbean. With the reduction in army numbers following the end of the Napoleonic Wars in 1815, many soldiers (especially those who had been slaves) from the disbanded 2nd and 4th West India Regiments were settled in Freetown. This deepened the ties between the community and its guardians, providing the colonial government with a pool of experienced volunteers for its militia.

GROWING PAINS
In 1821, Sierra Leone was added to a patchwork quilt of former Royal

ABOVE · *42nd (Highland) Regiment of Foot fight off an Ashanti ambush in West Africa.*

LEFT · *A soldier of the West India Regiment. Queen Victoria much admired the uniforms of the French colonial Zouaves and insisted on a North African-style dress for her Caribbean infantry.*

THE ANGLO-ASHANTI WARS

The 1st Anglo-Ashanti War (1823-1826)

British conflict with the Ashanti Kingdom had been brewing ever since the two powers changed direction over the issues of slavery. In 1823, the Ashanti captured a British sergeant during their scrap with the Fante, a tribe allied with Britain. His execution and the need to secure Gold Coast's frontier started the 1st Anglo-Ashanti War (1823-1826).

The plan had been to join forces with three other columns, but on the afternoon of January 21, 1824, Governor Sir Charles MacCarthy advanced through the jungle and found himself facing the 10,000-strong Ashanti army. The British side was comprised of 170 Cape Coast Militia, 80 men of the unsavoury Royal African Corps, and 240 Fante warriors.

There was really no excuse for overconfidence, but MacCarthy was convinced the Ashanti would defect when faced with their obvious superiority and he ordered his band strike up *God Save the King*. They didn't defect, they attacked. The British had five boxes of ammunition, and when one ran out they discovered the other four contained macaroni. Wounded, MacCarthy shot himself rather than face capture and torture. Out of respect for his bravery during the Battle of Nsamankow, the Ashanti ate his heart, beheaded him and used the skull as a ritual drinking vessel.

The Ashanti then marched on Cape Coast Castle, but the new Gold Coast governor, John Hope Smith, raised an army of tribes hostile to the Ashanti and beat them in the field on August 7, 1826. A new boundary along the Pra River was agreed between the Fante and Ashanti.

The Ashanti invasion is finally repulsed by a naval party from HMS Barracuda.

The 2nd Anglo-Ashanti War (1863-1864)

While the Dutch had paid the Ashanti a tribute, once their Gold Coast slave forts were acquired by the British, they had no intention of honouring this agreement. Tensions were running high, and in December 1863 a large Ashanti force crossed the frontier in pursuit of a fugitive. Defeating all the tribes they encountered as they pushed on through the jungle to the coast, the Ashanti were finally checked by a detachment of Royal Marine Light Infantry landed from HMS *Barracuda*.

The 3rd Anglo-Ashanti War (1873-1874)

Over the intervening decade of acrimonious contact between the Ashanti Kingdom and the Gold Coast Colony, the British

Britain's liberal reformers believed passionately that if slavery were eradicated throughout Africa, the incentives would exist for trade in other resources to thrive. Unlike slavery, this trade would create vibrant local economies which in turn would create markets for British businesses. If these other resources happened to be untapped mineral wealth, then British businesses would be doubly blessed by importing iron ore and exporting textiles and teapots in return.

The poster boy for this view was the Scottish missionary and explorer David Livingstone (1813-1873). Undeniably daring and immeasurably popular, his reports from the African interior shaped Britain's view of the continent and the solution to its 'problems', namely, his mantra of "Christianity, civilisation and commerce."

African Company forts (parts of modern Gambia, Ghana and Nigeria) to form British West Africa. Its boundaries continued to expand, as under pressure from the abolitionists in parliament they purchased the Danish slave forts in 1850, and then the Dutch forts in 1872.

This moral mission drove Britain not just to upbraid its European counterparts, but to expand its influence in Africa. Thanks to the demand in the Spanish Americas, Brazil, and across the Muslim world, many West African rulers had grown rich selling off their enemies and their unwanted, and they wished to remain rich. The Ashantehene, the King of the Ashanti, had no intention of ending his role in the slave trade, asking of the British: "If they think it is bad now, why did they think it was good before?"

The result was an on-off Anglo-Ashanti War that extended Britain's imperial possessions further inland, and it was just one of many. In 1851, the refusal of Lagos to end its role in the slave trade resulted in a naval bombardment and the raising of the Union flag, formally becoming the Colony of Lagos in 1862. Where possible, the British government preferred economic rather than hard power, but the result was the same - an empire grew in small steps.

In northeast Africa, Isma'il Pasha, the Khedive of Egypt and Sudan, was nearing bankruptcy. His attempts to reform the Egyptian army along European lines and then go to war with Ethiopia had drawn him deeper into Britain's debt. He ⟫

LEFT · The Ashanti open fire with their muskets on the British infantry advancing through the jungle.

government debated how best to respond to bring their belligerent neighbour to heel.

Heat and disease had led to the Gold Coast being dubbed 'white man's grave', and there was little appetite for an expeditionary force. Colonel Sir Garnet Wolseley was tasked to draw up plans and taking a clique of 36 British officers - later known as 'the Ashanti Ring' - he raised a professional army from the African levies and sent Lieutenant Colonel Evelyn Wood to negotiate with local chiefs to form an anti-Ashanti alliance.

With the introduction of quinine to the British Army, the swamps and jungles would no longer shield the Ashanti from the advance of empire. The bark of Peruvian cinchona tree had been used by the Spanish to treat fevers from as early as the 1570s (and by indigenous people for far longer), but it was only in 1820 that the active ingredient, quinine, was isolated. Incredibly expensive, the growth of British settlement in malaria-rich climates drove a need for mass production and from the 1860s a network of cinchona plantations were established. Spearheaded by the 42nd (Highland) Regiment of Foot, on January 24, 1874 the Battle of Amoaful inflicted a decisive defeat on the Ashanti and the British were free to march to the capital, Kumasi. They set the city alight, demolished the Azomethane's palace with explosives, and gawped in horror at the 'Death Grove', packed with the remains 120,000 sacrificial victims.

In the ensuring Treaty of Fomena, the Asantehene agreed to pay the British 50,000 ounces of gold, renounce supremacy over

42nd (Highland) Regiment of Foot advance through the jungle in 1874, the first time the British successfully waged war in the African interior.

several the frontier tribes, waive rent payments on the forts, grant free passage on all roads, and end human sacrifice.

THE CAPE FRONTIER WARS

ABOVE · *White officers serving with Mfengu units pose with their gruesome Xhosa trophies.*

ABOVE · *The Loyal Fingo by Thomas Baines shows a column of Mfengu irregulars in the Cape Frontier Wars.*

A series of nine conflicts fought over 100 years between 1779 and 1879, the Cape Frontier Wars - or Xhosa Wars - were a quagmire of shifting territories and factions too complex to cover in detail. The first three Frontier Wars were fought between the migrating Boers and Xhosa as they sought to settle the matter of borders.

British ownership of Cape Colony brought complaints about Xhosa raids on Boer settlements to the attention of the governor. British objectives were an optimistic dream of Pax Romana, they sought to not only secure their own frontier but to establish their authority over the Boers. British involvement changed the character of the Frontier Wars from a series of raids and retaliations by armed settlers, into campaigns by professional infantry.

At the end of the 4th Frontier War, Lieutenant General John Cradock reported to his satisfaction that "there has not

been shed more [Xhosa] blood than would seem necessary to impress on the minds of these savages a proper degree of terror and respect."

The Frontier Wars pushed the borders of Cape Colony further east and the new lands were administered as British Kaffraria with a regional capital at King William's Town. British Kaffraria was part tribal reservation and part border march, settled by both white farmers and Mfengu. The Mfengu, or 'Fingoes', were an ethnic group traditionally hostile to Xhosa, and they established farms and fought as irregulars for the Cape Colony.

As the nature of the war changed, the Xhosa fell under the thrall of prophets preaching syncretistic blends of Christianity and indigenous beliefs. This culminated in the greatest act of mass self-harm in southern Africa. Following the 8th Frontier War, Nongqawuse emerged with answers for the string of defeats. She proclaimed that if the Xhosa destroyed their crops and killed their cattle, the dead would rise and sweep the British into the sea. The resulting famine saw 40,000 die of starvation and others turn to cannibalism, with parents reported to have turned on their own children.

The 9th Frontier War was the last, but it began a new chapter in southern Africa's colonial conflict. Tensions inflamed by a recent drought, Mfengu and Xhosa were coming to blows, and the newly installed governor of Cape Colony and High Commissioner for Native Affairs, Sir Henry Bartle Frere, thought it was about time that the last independent Xhosa Kingdom, Griqualand, be annexed to British Kaffraria.

Frere wanted to bring in British troops and he wanted the Cape Colony to carry the cost. Cape Colony's prime minister John Molteno, meanwhile, was reluctant to involve London. Recently semi-autonomous from Britain, the constitution of Cape Colony was ill-defined, and Frere successfully ousted Molteno from office. Frere had his blank cheque and was sent several men who would go on to form the backbone of the disastrous first stage of the Anglo-Zulu War.

ABOVE · *A Khoikhoi sergeant of the Cape Mounted Rifles, one of the many irregular companies that fought in the Frontier Wars against the Xhosa.*

and the British government, many British companies continued to play a role in the illicit sale of Africans. This was not just through parts of the coast free of British writ, but through British West Africa itself. The situation on the ground was often messy, with governors dependent on powerful merchant companies and other influential local interests. It was often more conducive for the smooth-running of cash-strapped administrations for the governor and his staff to turn a blind eye. For as long as the demand existed, some Britons were prepared to cater for it, and complicity in the flow of slaves from West Africa continued well beyond the 1870s.

THE BOERS AND BANTU

At the time of European exploration of southern Africa, this rich and fertile land was sparsely populated by the pastoral people now collectively referred to as Khoisan. The name is a compound of Khoikhoi (or Khoekhoen), and the Sān (or Sākhoen), and they subsisted as herdsmen or hunter-gathers. The Boers called them, simply and derogatively, Hottentots and Bushmen.

Arab merchants had left a network of trading posts along the coast of the Cape of Good Hope that were used by the Portuguese in the 15th century. The first maritime power to attempt to navigate around Africa following the closure of the overland route to Asia, for the Portuguese this wild coast was a way-station to the spice-rich East.

As the Dutch supplanted the Portuguese as the apex predator of the Age of Exploration, the mercantile Dutch East India Company took over the ring of trading posts and ports of the newly formed Cape Colony. This small community of Dutch settlers, joined by a minority of German mercenaries and

agreed to end the slave trade through his territory and in 1870 he appointed British General Charles George Gordon governor-general of Sudan with the mandate to end the flow of slaves. In 1875 as his financial woes deepened, he sold Egypt's shares in the Suez Canal Company to the

British government (giving them a 44% stake), and in 1877 was forced to accept constitutional reform and appoint British finance minister to his cabinet.

The bitter irony is that although the slave trade was much reduced in West Africa by the actions of the Royal Navy

French Huguenots, grew without official encouragement to become the ancestors of the Afrikaners. With the Dutch East India Company offering little support, the settlers saw no reason to recognise the authority of the Cape Colony.

Venturing further and further inland, they set up vast farms in this largely untouched wilderness and developed a hardy self-reliance even by the standards of frontier settlers in Australia or North America. The Boers, as the farmers called themselves, were an authority unto themselves and the thinly spread Khoisan - who they referred to collectively as 'kaffirs' (meaning 'infidel', a legacy of the earlier Arab presence) - were easy pickings. Many were forced to work in conditions little better than slavery alongside chattel slaves imported from the Dutch territories in Angola, Madagascar and the East Indies.

Recalling his first visit to Cape Colony in 1800, Sir John Barrow wrote: "The Boer, notwithstanding, has his enjoyments, he is absolute master of a domain of several miles in extent; and he lords it over a few miserable slaves or Hottentots without control."

THE BRITISH IN CAPE COLONY

The 1815 Congress of Vienna and Treaty of Paris, which followed the defeat of Napoleon Bonaparte, cemented a stable new order for the great empires of Europe but also presented Britain with an opportunity to secure its maritime pre-eminence. The

BELOW · *The Royal Navy take control of the Cape of Good Hope from the Dutch, 1806.*

territorial changes of the last two decades of conflict had deepened Britain's toehold in India and its strategic interests were best served by controlling the Cape of Good Hope and increasing its presence in the Indian Ocean. The latter served by the former French islands of Mauritius and Seychelles.

After a short battle in 1806, the Dutch East India Company surrendered Cape Colony to Britain and the Congress of Vienna made that permanent. Of its population of 60,000, 27,000 were white, 17,000 free Khoikhoi, and 16,000 slaves. Insistence on a collective fight against the slave trade had been added to the Treaty of Paris by the British delegation, and the total ban on owning slaves within the British Empire came into force 15 years later.

Where the Dutch administration left the settlers to their own devices, the British were more involved. Their interactions with indigenous peoples were shaped by the consolidation of rule in India. They instinctively adopted the same model based around collaboration with local leaders, careful adherence to local traditions, a 'fair' application of the rule of law, and the basic improvement of conditions.

The aim of the colonial governments was for the constitute peoples to live together harmoniously, content that their far-off monarch had made them happier and healthier. Most Boers meanwhile viewed Africa as a promised land to be claimed and their intense brand of Calvinism viewed Africans as the cursed descendants of Noah's

grandson, Canaan. This was the traditional explanation for black skin in those parts of the Christian and Muslim world that sought moral justification for slavery in the scriptures.

To a lesser extent, the British came to view the civilising mission of empire as extending to the Boers as well, who they thought as uncouth and backwards. As British authority crept from Cape Town to the farmsteads, the Boers moved further northeast to keep them at arm's length.

The migrating Boers - called Trekboer - collided with the Xhosa migration from the opposite direction. The Xhosa were part of the larger Bantu people who originated in west and central Africa and they couldn't have been more different from the Khoisan. Xhosa wasn't the name they called themselves, it meant 'fierce' in the Sān language.

Unlike the small family groups of Khoisan, the Xhosa were organised into larger clans under a single chieftain and were not so easily broken, sparking a series of on-off frontier conflicts that lasted a century. The Boer interactions with the Xhosa, transformed frontier life into one of constant violence and dragged Britain further inland to protect its missionaries and merchants, take charge of disputed resources, and pacify restive tribes.

Among the other Bantu tribes who found themselves competing with the Boers and the British, were the Basotho, the Mfengu, the Swazi, and, of course, the Zulu. ◀◀◀

A State of WAR

The Rise of the Zulu

A Bantu warrior preparing to throw his assegai, he holds a bundle of extra spears in his free hand. Illustrated by Thomas J Lucas for his 1861 book, Pen and Pencil Reminiscences of a Campaign in South Africa.

ABOVE · *An example of a modest Bantu kraal at the time of the First Boer War in 1900, although the layout would have been little changed from the reign of Shaka.*

The Anglo-Zulu War of 1879 was at its heart a collision of imperial powers. Over six decades what had begun as a minor tribe had become a ruthless warrior state whose conquests had resulted in vast columns of refugees leaving their lands for the shelter of British Cape Colony and made them the master of the only resource that really mattered to Boer and Bantu alike - cattle.

What's more, the Zulu Kingdom remained stubbornly unbowed by contact with white settlers, repeatedly putting the pugnacious Boers firmly in their place and reaching an uneasy peace with the Cape Colony that would soon implode under the weight of Britain's African ambitions. The fierce warrior culture that the British went to war with - fetishized by 19th century writers as "black Spartans" - was largely the product of a man born over a century earlier. Like many warrior kings of history - from William the Conqueror to Charlemagne - Shaka kaSenzangakhona, or Shaka Zulu, was illegitimate. As such he was destined to either fight or fail - there were no half measures.

Shaka was born in 1787 to Senzangakhona kaJama - chief of the Zulu - and the woman who would eventually become the third (and least) of the chief's 16 wives, Nandi kaBhebhe. She was the daughter of a Langeni chief and to try averting scandal the Zulu elders blamed her unwelcome pregnancy on Nandi having an intestinal beetle - or 'shaka' - and the name stuck.

Nandi and Senzangakhona weren't married at the time of the conception and Nandi's family demanded damages. Senzangakhona paid them 50 cattle to offset his transgression, and both mother and child were welcomed into the chief's kraal.

A kraal was a configuration common among the Bantu. Usually located near fresh water and land suitable for grazing, it was a village arranged as a ring of single storey huts around a large open cattle pen where the herd spent the night and were brought in for milking at midday. There was a strict hierarchy of hut placement, with the chief's wives surrounding the cattle pen in order of importance.

Usually, the chief's heir came from one of his later wives who would be designated the Great Wife, and there was no expectation that Shaka would have inherited his father's throne under any circumstances. Being the first male child of a chief made him a threat in the Bantu succession as having a son reach adulthood while a chief was still in his prime was to effectively groom your own usurper. ⟫⟫⟫

LEFT · *A sketch of Shaka by an unknown European artist, appearing in Nathanial Isaacs's Travels and Adventures in Eastern Africa, 1836. Though Isaacs met Shaka, no images are known to exist from his lifetime.*

The reign of a chief was generally short and violent, and it was probably Shaka's illegitimacy that spared him from having his brains bashed out as an infant.

THE MAKING OF A WARRIOR

Never accepted by the Zulu, Nandi was outspoken and forthright, and after attacking one of Senzangakhona's headmen with an iWisa - a club with a hefty ball on the end - the two were kicked out and sent to live with her tribe, the Lageni.

Shaka had inherited his mother's volatile temperament. He soon quarrelled with the son of the Lageni's current chief and was cast out again, this time to live with a Lageni sub-tribe, the Mthethwa. There Shaka's aggression found a home and he was used as a warrior in the service of the Mthethwa chief Jobe, and then his son and successor Dingiswayo - who fulfilled the reputation of his name, 'The Troubled One.'

Before Dingiswayo and Shaka's military reforms, tribal conflicts in southwestern Africa were a matter of short and theatrical skirmishes that left few dead but settled the pecking order, allowing tribes to absorb each other, splinter off, or reform.

Boys of the same age grew up, played, and tended their herds together in an iNtanga. The lifestyle of the Bantu was a hard one - even for infants, who were subject to rituals designed to strengthen them such as being buried up to their necks in the earth, being smoked over a fire, and having reeds

inserted into their rectums until they bled. Those who survived to adolescence were tough young men, they were issued with six-foot throwing spears, and in times of war would be formed into an ad-hoc army called an iMpi.

Dingiswayo, whose taste for innovation extended to riding a horse and carrying a gun taken from a white settler, treated each crop of iNtanga as an iButho-in-training - calling up successive drafts of young warriors to serve in amaButho regiments in his army. It was into this dynamic new system, and under an equally dynamic new chief that Shaka came of age.

Dingiswayo brought neighbouring tribes to heel, replaced their chiefs with client rulers who were promptly married into his family, and then drafted their young into his amaButho system. It was a form of imperialism unknown to the Bantu, and soon the reputation of the Mthethwa alone was enough to bring rival chiefs to the negotiating table without bloodshed. For Dingiswayo war was a means to an end so this was ideal, but for Shaka conquest was meaningless if the foe retained the strength to one day turn on their conqueror.

Shaka led his regiment with absolute brutality. He would press an advantage to excess, decimating his enemies and incorporating their scattered survivors into the amaButho, making it one of the most feared fighting forces in Dingiswayo's domain. Dissatisfied with the traditional

assegai throwing spear, Shaka devised a shorter stabbing spear, the iKlwa, which made better use of his gift for close-quarter fighting. He even turned the cow skin shield into a weapon of war, using it to twist his opponent's shield to one-side and expose his torso or armpit to the warrior's wicked blade. Shaka also fought barefoot, which allowed him greater speed and agility than his sandal-clad comrades.

RECLAIMING HIS BIRTHRIGHT

Eventually, the Zulu were absorbed into the Mthethwa Empire and Dingiswayo began to groom his champion as the potential chief of his estranged father's tribe. In the meantime, Shaka continued his reforms: he finessed his techniques with the iKlwa and took the emphasis off the throwing spears in favour of a brutal charge at the enemy, training his men to drop into a crouch and hold their shields at just the right angle to send incoming assegai glancing off harmlessly.

He also birthed his signature battle tactic - the 'Horns of the Buffalo'. The regiment were separated into three parts; first, the men in the centre (the chest) would charge the enemy and hold them in a bloody close-quarter melee, then the left and right flanks (the horns) would encircle their entrapped enemy. Crucially, Shaka understood the value of love as well as fear, and he passed most of the cattle given to him by Dingiswayo onto the men of his amaButho.

In 1816, word reached Dingiswayo that

British Land Pattern Musket (Brown Bess)

A shorter Brown Bess carbine, used by British cavalry. ANTIQUE MILITARY RIFLES CC BY-SA 2.0

The British Army's standard issue muzzle-loading black powder flintlock from 1722 until 1838, it was as ubiquitous on the early 19th century battlefield as the Kalashnikov is today. Its simple, standardised pattern meant that it could be copied, modified and repaired with ease, and could be acquired by a Zulu warrior in exchange for a sheep or goat - the lowest unit of Bantu coinage.

The target needed to be 100 yards away at most for the Brown Bess to have any real chance of hitting them, and while the British used tightly packed mass volleys to offset the low effective range, the Zulu used muskets for harassing fire and preferred to do their fighting hand-to-hand.

IWisa Club

A weighted club common across southern and eastern Africa and often known by its generic name of knobkerrie, the iWisa was cut from a single piece of hardwood about 18 inches long, while the weighted ball varied from four to seven inches across.

A brutal bludgeon capable of shattering a human skull with a single blow, the iWisa was often used in executions and mercy killings as well as warfare. Versatile as well as deadly, the iWisa could also be thrown spinning through the air towards its target.

ETNOGRAFISKA MUSEET CC BY 2.5

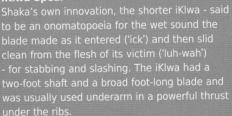

IKlwa Spear

Shaka's own innovation, the shorter iKlwa - said to be an onomatopoeia for the wet sound the blade made as it entered ('ick') and then slid clean from the flesh of its victim ('luh-wah') - for stabbing and slashing. The iKlwa had a two-foot shaft and a broad foot-long blade and was usually used underarm in a powerful thrust under the ribs.

A Zulu warrior poses with an iKlwa stabbing spear and an iWisa club from the 1917 travelogue, The Lure of Africa

LEFT · *Utimuni, nephew of Shaka, depicted in an 1849 book, The Kafirs Illustrated. Utimuni's elaborate dress is a good example of the uniforms worn by the iMpi in ceremonial settings to foster regimental pride.*

Senzangakhona had died and Shaka's half-brother, Sigujana had taken the throne. Shaka was given permission to return to the Zulu royal kraal and secure his birthright. When the 29-year old warlord arrived to meet the people he had not broken bread with since he was six, he found his ruthless reputation had preceded him - the Zulu had murdered their new ruler and dumped him in a stream.

Using summary execution to bring his terrified new tribe into line (and settle some personal scores), Shaka was now able to test his military innovations on a larger scale. He added a fourth contingent to his Horns of the Buffalo, a reserve (the loins) that would be seated behind the centre to preserve their energy (and stop them getting carried away and joining in prematurely).

He arranged all fighting age men into amaButho with the youngest age group forced to remain celibate and prevented from marrying until they had ten years of service behind them. They lived together in their own military kraal - a garrison town - as ⟫⟫

Assegai Spear

Bantu warriors generally fought with a bundle of light throwing spears called assegai. Prior to Shaka, tribes would generally fight by keeping their distance and hurling volley after volley of spears back and forth. Under Shaka's leadership, the Zulu loosed one volley to soften up their targets before charging.

IsiHlangu Shield

An oval-shaped cow skin shield was core to the Zulu warrior's fighting style. They were kept in the kraal's armoury and issued before the battle. Junior regiments carried black shields, and veteran regiments of mostly married men carried white or red shields.

Shields came in different sizes, with the larger isiHlangu (meaning 'sweep aside') used to parry an opponent's weapon - a tactic that proved as effective in seeing off British bayonets as it did a rival tribe's war clubs - or knock them off balance. Standing four to six feet tall, the isiHlangu's cowhide pattern could be used for camouflage allowing men to infiltrate alongside herds of cattle.

A depiction of a kraal in flames and a tribe massacring its neighbours in the trauma of the Mfecane, which left as many as two million Africans dead.

ABOVE · *Dingane orders the slaughter of the Boer delegation, depicted here as being stabbed by spears in the kraal. In fact, they were bludgeoned with clubs on a hill overlooking the Zulu capital.*

between the powerful Mthethwa and their rivals, and he called on Shaka frequently to join his military campaigns.

For religious reason, these campaigns were short and sharp. If a Bantu warrior slew his foe he risked going insane and a malady settling upon his cattle unless he then slashed open the dead man's stomach to release his spirit. He would then journey back to his home kraal and eat and sleep apart from his brethren until the spiritual cleansing at the hands of his witch doctor was complete. In terms of combat effectiveness this meant that following a battle, large numbers of veteran warriors

> "SHAKA WAS THE SOLE RULER BY RIGHT OF CONQUEST AND HIS DESTRUCTION OF RIVALS SUNDERED THE OLD TRIBAL LOYALTIES UNTIL THOSE WHO LIVED UNDER THE ZULU YOKE BEGAN TO IDENTIFY AS ZULU THEMSELVES."

the heart of his new army, the prototype for each successive wave of new Zulu warriors.

He drilled the Zulu mercilessly in their new combat techniques. On pain of death, they were forced to shed their sandals and march over thorns to toughen their soles until they were said to be able to cover 50 miles in a single day. He nominated boys too young to fight to follow the iMpi with water and grain to keep them provisioned, and he inspired a passionate esprit de corps, with each amaButho having a distinct uniform of feathered

headdresses and animal pelts, their own battle cry, and their own song.

As the regiments grew and absorbed their defeated rivals (including the Lageni, which enabled Shaka to settle a few more scores on his and his mother's behalf), they formed sub-iMpi - effectively becoming brigades. Highly mobile, impeccably drilled, devoted to their king, and masters of close-quarter fighting, the Zulu were capable of taking on clans of far greater numbers. Dingiswayo was content for the Zulu to expand on his distant frontier, providing a valuable buffer

ABOVE · *A simplified depiction of the layout of a larger kraal, with the cattle stockade in the centre doubling up as a meeting space and parade ground. Calves were kept in the enclosure at the back of the central stockade, and directly behind it was the hut of the chief's Great Wife.*

would peel away from the iMpi and walk home. It wasn't a huge problem in tribal conflicts where both sides paid the same spiritual toll, but devastating when Bantu found themselves in prolonged engagements with white foes.

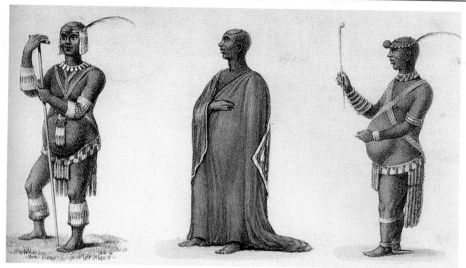

ABOVE · *Depictions of Digane in his normal robes and ceremonial dress by Captain Allen Francis Gardiner. Published in his Narrative of a Journey to the Zulu Country in South Africa, undertaken in 1835 and 1836, Gardiner met with the king multiple times.*

THE PRICE OF EMPIRE

Dingiswayo's death in 1817 - he was captured and beheaded by Zwide, chief of the Ndwandwe - left a power vacuum that Shaka charged into with abandon. He waged war on the larger Ndwandwe who by then had adopted a crude copy of the iKwla and were no easy mark.

More than a brute who hammered his enemies into submission, at the Battle of Mhlatuze River in 1819, Shaka arranged his smaller army on a hill to confront the larger Ndwandwe force. He kept his reserve hidden in a depression and drew away part of the Ndwandwe army by making a show of leading the Zulu cattle away from the battlefield. It was a costly exchange despite Shaka's cunning, but the Ndwandwe were driven away and their royal kraal butchered in a sneak attack.

The Zulu Empire that Shaka had built was a completely different beast from Dingiswayo's confederation of client chiefs and tribes. Shaka was the sole ruler by right of conquest and his destruction of rivals sundered the old tribal loyalties until those who lived under the Zulu yoke began to identify as Zulu themselves.

In 1816 when Shaka took the throne,

Zululand was a territory of a hundred or so miles around his dead father's kraal and an army of 350 warriors. By the 1820s it stretched 11,500 square miles from the coast to the Blood River in the west, and from Pongola River in the north to the Tugela River in the south, and Shaka could call up 20,000 fighting men.

Shaka was a warlord first and a king second. Oral histories and Bantu folklore speak of his cruelty, his summary executions of those who displeased him for the most trivial of offenses, and he ordered constant raids on his neighbours for no economic or territorial gain - simply bloodlust. He fathered no children - or at least allowed no children to survive - having seen what even an exiled bastard is capable of.

Following the hysterical reaction to the death of his mother Nandi in 1827, the rest of his family decided they had seen enough of King Shaka the Great. Up to 7,000 mourners were massacred and the queen mother was buried with ten handmaidens to keep her company - all ten were still alive, having had their legs broken. He ordered that any woman who fell pregnant would be executed and ordered that no crops be planted for a year - he rescinded these edicts after three months, mindful that he had gone too far.

While his army were fighting elsewhere on September 24, 1828, Shaka's half-brother Mhlangana walked calmly up to him and stabbed him in the shoulder. Shaka turned around in confusion and was stabbed again, this time in the side. The king died from a flurry of blows from his own creation, the iKwla, aged 41.

Another half-brother, Dingane kaSenzangakhona, emerged from the conspiracy as King of the Zulus, having stabbed Mhlangana for the privilege.

The effect of years of brutal, seemingly ceaseless warfare was catastrophic. Rather than fight, many tribes simply packed up their kraals and fled their homelands for safe havens that didn't exist, their flight sending them crashing into other tribal territories creating a domino effect of war and migration. Europeans also played a role in this escalating horror. Boxed in by British and Boer settlements south of the Orange River, and the Portuguese in the northeast, west was the only direction for displaced Bantu to go.

The fight for survival was bitter and for the most part, Europeans were

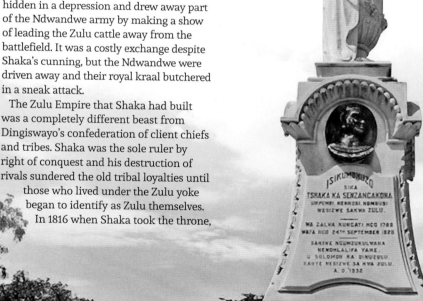

A monument to Shaka, honouring his role as the founder of the modern Zulu Nation, marks his grave in Stangar, KwaZulu-Natal. It was erected in 1932 and folklore holds that a nearby rock is where the king was sitting when he was assassinated. JRAMATSUI CC BY-SA 3.0

oblivious to what was unfolding over the next ridge. Across the first half of the 1800s the Mfecane - the Crushing' - spread across southern Africa and as many as two million people were killed in the chaos. Some resorted to cannibalism, huge swathes of the country were depopulated, and columns of refugees even reached the limits of British and Boer settlement.

When the Voortrekkers travelled north, they found a near-empty landscape on which only decades earlier tribes had grazed their cattle and grown their crops. The Boers had found their 'lekker lewe', the 'sweet life', where they could work the soil and tend their herds far from the interference of the British colonial authorities, but they now had some very dangerous neighbours.

THE BEST OF ENEMIES

British ownership of the 100-square mile Cape Colony was ratified by the 1815 Congress of Vienna which dictated the world order in the wake of Napoléon's defeat at Waterloo. Britain immediately

ABOVE · A copy of the 1838 treaty between Retief and Dingane. It was written in English and grants the Voortrekkers ownership of the land, which is a concept unheard of in Bantu society - land remained property of the tribe regardless of who occupied it.

embarked on a far more hands-on administration than the settlers were used to. Faced with taxation, the use of English rather than Dutch for official business, the prosecution of Boers for beating their African servants, and a ban on slavery, a tenth of the colony's white population - 14,000 Boers in all - began the 'Great Trek' north in 1835, piling their families and belongings into ox-drawn wagons.

One trek leader, Piet Retief, set his sights on Natal and opened negotiations with Dingane for permission to settle, while the Orange Free State and the Transvaal Republic were settled to the Zulu's west and northwest. Boer encounters with the Bantu in the Frontier Wars had convinced them that Africans posed little threat to these hardy farmers with their muskets and their horses, and Retief boasted to the Zulu king of the tribes they had laid low on the way north.

Dingane viewed these new arrivals with growing insecurity. Their tales of victory over his southern neighbours left him concerned that they were the advance guard of a larger invasion force, and when

A depiction of a Zulu attack on a Boer camp in 1838, the year of the Retief massacre, by Charles Davidson Bell. Bell held several posts in the Cape Colony and put his artistic skills to official use creating postage stamps, heraldry and medals.

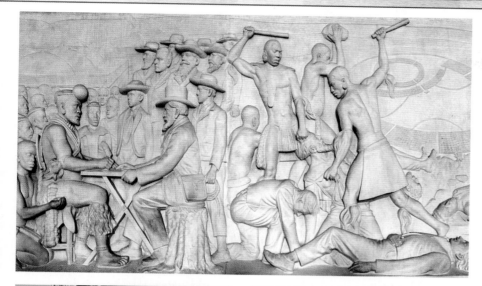

the Battle of Blood River on December 16, 1838, 64 wagons were formed into a circle and - aided by an artillery piece - the 600 defenders fired volley after volley into the attacking Zulu as they charged, killing thousands of warriors and suffering only four wounded in return. Finally, Shaka's disdain for ranged weapons decades earlier had cost his kingdom dearly. Confronted with what they viewed as a divinely ordained triumph, in 1839 the victorious Voortrekkers founded the Natalia Republic and its capital Pietermaritzburg.

This crushing defeat sealed Dingane's fate. His half-brother, Mpande kaSenzangakhona, gathered 17,000 followers and marched to Natalia for support. The stunned Boers took advantage of this latest round of fratricidal feeling among the Zulu royal family and agreeing to honour Mpande's claim to the throne, urged him back to Zululand with a Boer commando for support. Dingane fled and after his followers gradually peeled off and left their disgraced king, he was murdered anonymously in a forest.

Britain had been watching all of this closely and wasn't best pleased.

During Shaka's lifetime, careful diplomatic overtures to the Zulu had resulted in an independent British settlement at Port Natal (renamed Durban in 1835), and more recently Dingane had signed a treaty with Britain. With the situation clearly out of control in Natalia, the jittery Cape Colony dispatched soldiers to restore a manageable status quo.

They took direct control of Durban and brought the nascent republic of Natalia reluctantly under the union flag by force, forming the British Colony of Natal in 1844.

By the second half of the 19th century, these mutually suspicious entities faced each other over uncertain borders. During the 9th Frontier War the British Cape Colony had advanced into Xhosa lands until it reached the Orange Free State, which in turn shared frontiers with Zululand and British Natal, as well as the Transvaal Republic.

Zululand had white settlers on three sides and the ocean on another. In time, Mpande's son and successor would fight with his back to the wall. ◀◀◀

ABOVE · *The names of Piet Reteif and the men killed on Execution Hill, overlooking the Zulu royal kraal, adorns this memorial, which was erected in 1922.* JMK CC BY-SA 3.0

ABOVE · *Mpande at leisure. The third Zulu king owed his reign to the Boers and was the least impressive of their number, although he did preside over a period of relative peace in the region.*

a number of wagons prematurely entered Zulu territory he took this as confirmation. Dingane cautiously granted Retief permission to settle, tasked the Boer with recovering some cattle that had been stolen as a gesture of goodwill, and invited him and his men back to finalise their treaty.

When Retief returned from besting Dingane's cattle thief he confirmed the king's anxiety with a show of force at the royal kraal, galloping around the stockade the Boer commando fired their rifles into the air. Dingane put his mark on Retief's contract and then murdered the entire Boer party over breakfast. With around 100 men executed one-by-one while the struggling Retief watched, Dingane then dispatched three regiments of Zulu to take care of the Boers waiting patiently for Retief's deal to be signed in their laagers (encampments of circled wagons).

The slaughter was indiscriminate. Striking in the dead of night, the Zulu killed 41 men, 56 women, 185 children and 250 black servants. The Boers retaliated with a 347-man commando, supported by Boer settlers from the nearby Orange Free State. Fiercely independent, overall Boer command of the punishment raid was non-existent. The commando was lured into a battlefield of Dingane's choosing, encircled by an 8,000-strong Zulu force, and forced to withdraw.

Learning from their experience, the Boers began to make stronger use of their laagers and concentrated firepower. At

BEATING THE DRUMS

Provoking War with the Zulu

In October 1872 Mpande kaSenzangakhona, King of the Zulu, died aged 74. His passing sealed a remarkable era; Mpande was the longest reigning Zulu monarch who presided over a largely unbroken period of peace; he had died of old age and not violence; and for the first time the Zulu throne was passed to a nephew and not a brother of the Zulu Kingdom's blood-soaked founder, Shaka kaSenzangakhona.

Cetshwayo kaMpande was like his infamous uncle: the eldest son by the king's first wife and therefore ineligible for the succession. With King Mpande yet to designate a Great Wife, Cetshwayo was in a state of almost constant rivalry with his younger brother, Mbulazi, who was the king's favourite and as a result, had the surest claim in lieu of an official heir.

Mpande was a weak ruler, but that weakness had mostly brought about tranquillity as Zulu communities were left to govern themselves. Without firm central authority to bring them in line, Cetshwayo and Mbulazi gathered power bases and followers in a manner that would have been impossible under the cruel and paranoid Shaka the Great.

These factions were formal enough to have names - uSuthu (from the Zulu war cry "We have eaten") and iziGqoza (meaning "to drip like water from the roof", reflecting the trickle of followers to Mbulazi's banner), respectively - and in 1856 they went to war. Too late and too weak to make a difference, Mpande threw his support behind his favourite.

With 7,000 iziGqoza warriors to 20,000 uSuthu, Mbulazi gathered up his loyalists and their kraals - some 20,000 to 30,000 refugees in all - and fled for the Tugela River which marked the natural border with the Colony of Natal where they were met by Captain Joshua Walmsley, a Natal Border Agent. Walmsley had no desire to get involved and was even less enthusiastic about the prospect of a bloody civil war on Natal's porous frontier.

He turned the iziGqoza back. Their slaughter was total and for decades the site was marked by a white smear

ABOVE · *Young Zulu warriors pose with their weapons, the iKwla stabbing spear and the iWisa club. It was easy to convince policy makers far from the field of the Zulu Kingdom's hostile intentions.*

of thousands upon thousands of bleached bones. Mbulazi was flayed alive and crucified on an ant hill.

THE MAN WHO WOULD BE KING

Over almost 70 years as custodian of southern Africa between 1795 and 1872, Britain had found its frontiers constantly expanding in the spirit of belligerent paternalism, believing that both Boers and Bantu needed to be protected from themselves and each other.

A polyglot who spent his formative years in Africa, Theophilus Shepstone was Cape Colony's frontier fixer-at-large and had brought Natal into the imperial fold in 1838. Now Secretary for Native Affairs, his priority was to replicate the favourable relationship the colony had enjoyed with the docile Mpande with his unpredictable heir apparent. What little power the old king held had been eroded to mere symbolism by the 2nd Zulu Civil War that produced Cetshwayo's victory and British influence in Zululand had vanished along with it.

Cetshwayo was now waiting for his father to die. He kept close tabs on his siblings

and on the more autonomous chiefs who had grown too strong under Mpande's anaemic rule, butchering those who looked like potential challengers. One infant half-brother was swung violently against a tree until his skull shattered.

Shepstone acted quickly to earn Cetshwayo's favour. He travelled to the royal kraal at Nodwengu with a small party to entreat with Mpande and invited Cetshwayo to bear witness. In a grand gesture, Shepstone proclaimed Cetshwayo king-in-waiting in the name of King Mpande and Queen Victoria. The wily diplomat browbeat Mpande with all the charisma of a snake oil salesman and getting carried away gave a pompous speech to remind Cetshwayo to behave himself.

Cetshwayo was not so easily cowed. He appreciated the gesture of arranging his succession, but more for the support that it implied from Natal than the clearing up of his status. He would be king one way or another, but the importance of the relationship with his white neighbours was beginning to register and so he set his jaw and suffered Shepstone's admonishment in silence.

SIR GARNET WOLSELEY.

SHORT SERVICE AND QUICK RETURNS.

ABOVE · *An 1882 Punch cartoon of Sir Garnet Wolseley, a man once described by Gilbert & Sullivan as "the very model of a modern major general." Here his record of dipping in and out of colonial affairs is lampooned.*

CONFEDERATION.

ABOVE · *An editorial cartoon from a Cape Colony newspaper hostile to confederation, depicts the policy as an act of conquest in 1878. The octopus is a recurring motif in propaganda, surfacing during both World Wars.*

When October 1872 arrived, Zululand's biggest problem wasn't Natal, but to the west and northwest in the Transvaal Republic, which claimed a thousand-square-mile strip of Zululand.

Shepstone, who was not above outright fabrication, claimed that the king had invited him to garrison the Disputed Territory as a buffer. Given Shepstone's own strategic obsession with containing the Boers, it's more likely he pushed this idea himself.

ABOVE · *A map of southeastern Africa on the eve of the Anglo-Zulu War, showing the Colony of Natal and Transvaal, the independent Orange Free State, and the independent Zululand.*

RIGHT · *Cetshwayo kaMpande, the last independent King of the Zulu, pictured in 1878. Despite his stature, he was a strong and healthy man who walked vast distances each day.*

Shepstone, imagining himself kingmaker, began to organise an elaborate coronation for Cetshwayo, commissioning a gaudy tinsel crown and red robes from the costume department of the travelling opera company. He acquired a marquee and two handsomely carved oak office chairs to serve as thrones.

Forming up four units of volunteer mounted infantry from Natal, a company of volunteer artillery drawing their polished cannon by ox, a brass band, and a horse-drawn barouche to serve as the royal carriage, the coronation party carried Cetshwayo to the royal kraal, where to his relief, he was accepted by his father's chieftains without challenge.

Shepstone placed his risible crown on the king's head and anointed him in the name of Queen Victoria. Overrating his own importance as he had done in the matter of succession, he then proclaimed the values under which he expected Cetshwayo to rule, demanding an end to the tribal warfare, no more executions without trial, and the confiscation of goods as a punishment for lesser crimes rather than death. In response to each condition, the chiefs responded "Vuma!" ("We agree!").

This ritual call and response was only ever that: a ritual.

ABOVE · *A painting of Cape Town in 1850, even then it was the most prosperous and most developed of the white colonies in southern Africa.*

LEFT · *The view down Plein Street, in the heart of Cape Town, 1870,*

Like the Orange Free State, Transvaal was an independent state settled by Boers, but it was a sparsely populated one, divided between a small urban British population in the capital Pretoria and a larger rural Afrikaner one.

West of the Orange Free State was (from 1873) the British colony of Griqualand West, formed with the sole intent of plundering the Kimberley diamond fields, and east of the Orange Free State was the Colony of Natal, administered independently of Cape Colony by a lieutenant-governor. To the north of Natal, of course, was Zululand. Uniquely, Natal had land specifically set aside for the Bantu to continue their tribal lifestyle - not a generous allocation but it better than the sweet nothing available under white rule elsewhere.

To build a nation, Carnarvon had to set about destroying them too. He was convinced that confederation could only be achieved once the Orange Free State and the Transvaal Republic were under British control, but also Natal needed to be persuaded that its 'native policy' wouldn't be adversely affected by union. The key to the whole enterprise was perhaps the hardest sell: Cape Colony needed to be convinced of the merits of having its wealth bled dry by burdensome backwaters, and its stability put at risk by belligerent Transvaal Boers or indigenous uprisings in Natal.

CREEPING CONFEDERATION

Zululand's fate was about to be decided by the broad-brush strokes of a government minister over 8,000 miles away.

After three decades in the heart of African colonial affairs, Theophilus Shepstone was a force unto himself and he knew better than any governor or minister what the future of southern Africa held. With his close friend, the energetic Bishop of Natal, John William Colenso, the two set off for London in 1874 for an audience with the new Secretary of State for the Colonies, Henry Herbert, 4th Earl of Carnarvon.

They had set out to challenge an outcome of some minor act of policy in Natal but found themselves subject to intense scrutiny by Carnarvon. He had a more pressing agenda for the provincials. The sanctimonious 'white man's burden' of the British Empire earlier in the century was a luxury afforded by full coffers. Carnarvon was keen that the colonies should start managing their own affairs and finances.

In 1867 the colonies of Canada, Nova Scotia and New Brunswick had been formed into one self-governing Dominion of Canada, and a bumpier process of confederation was underway in Australia, then formed of six separate and fiercely individualistic colonies.

The challenge in Africa was even greater than that faced by federalists in the Antipodes. Cape Colony was the largest and wealthiest. It had a constitution, a parliament and since 1872 had been administered by an elected prime minister who shared a poorly defined division of responsibility with the governor, who answered to the Colonial Office.

North of Cape Colony was the stable and prosperous Orange Free State, and north of that the more fragile Transvaal Republic, also called the South African Republic.

Well-dressed women gather bundles of sticks in Cape Colony, the wealthiest of the settler states in southern Africa.

ARCHITECTS OF WAR

Carnarvon relieved Sir Benjamin Pine from his sedentary semi-retirement as lieutenant-governor of Natal and dispatched the distinguished old warhorse and Ashanti War celebrity Major-General Sir Garnet Wolseley, KCMG, KCB to serve as confederation's man on the ground. With Shepstone bending his ear on all matters of southern Africa, Wolseley set about winning over Natal society with cheap champagne, lavish balls, and bullish rhetoric.

On his return to London in August 1875 he told Carnarvon that the biggest obstacle to a single state was the vulnerable frontier with Zululand, and the strident imperialist heaped praise on the Boer attitude to their black neighbours by "reducing them to manageable proportions" and advocated annexation.

Shepstone had assured him, that such a conquest would only require a few thousand soldiers and the Zulu would cheer their liberation from Cetshwayo, who was held to be a murderous tyrant. This wasn't true, but Shepstone's malarkey was a heady brew to the uninitiated.

Carnarvon was less than enamoured with the idea of a military expedition against the Zulu but saw an opportunity to bring the Transvaal into the family. Paradoxically, while the robust Orange Free State was open to talk confederation, the more vulnerable Transvaal saw a rosier future elsewhere and it gambled, using the one resource it had in abundance - land - to underwrite the costs of a railway that would link Pretoria to the Portuguese trading post of Delagoa Bay.

Discovering that the railway ran right through the territory of the BaPedi, who had long been their rivals for land and labour in the north, the Transvaal went to war. While the Afrikaners had the will to dig in to protect their farms, families and communities, the idea of being committed to war for political ends was miserable motivation. The campaign was an expensive humiliation that doomed the railway and left massive amounts of land in the hands of speculators.

With the republic facing complete economic collapse, Carnarvon empowered Shepstone to ride to Pretoria and take possession of Transvaal for the crown. There was plenty of grumbling, but little resistance - the government was discredited, the people were weary, and British businesses in the region were glad of some stability.

Turning his attention to the Cape, Carnarvon pleaded with the Sir Henry Bartle Frere to step into the role of governor of Cape Colony, with an additional sweeping mandate as High Commissioner of Native Affairs for South Africa

LEFT · *An 1878 Transvaal postage stamp with the image of Queen Victoria. A visible relic of the short-lived and highly unpopular rule of Shepstone.*

that allowed him to interfere in the business of the other colonies.

An enthusiastic administrator, Frere had had a glittering career in a variety of roles in British India and his crowning achievement was negotiating with the Sultan of Zanzibar to end the slave trade from the island. A post to Britain's African bedlam wasn't even a sideways step, but the midwifery of a single unified South Africa on the Canadian model appealed to him enormously. He arrived in Cape Town in April 1877 shortly after Shepstone and his escort raised the union flag over the Transvaal.

From the second he disembarked, Frere was assailed by lurid newspaper »»

An open cast diamond mine in Kimberley, in the British colony of Griqualand West. The first diamonds were found in the region in 1871 and the Orange Free State claimed ownership, but the territory was quickly occupied by Britain.

reports of Zulu atrocities against Christian missionaries. For the most part, these were completely invented by the pro-annexation brigade, but Frere turned to a man in the know for confirmation - Shepstone - and received it.

REOPENING OLD WOUNDS

As British administrator of Transvaal, Shepstone returned to the matter of the Disputed Territory with an altogether different agenda. At the time of Cetshwayo's pantomime coronation, it had been a useful way of checking Boer ambitions and he had backed the Zulu to the hilt, but now those Boer ambitions had been inherited by Britain.

Afrikaner resentment to his coup was growing. Old habits die hard and Shepstone conducted himself as he had among the Bantu, with arrogance and petulance. What's more, there was no obvious solution to the issue of land so popping the stitches on the Disputed Territory would open fresh pastures for the settlers and serve to rally public opinion around the administration.

Cetshwayo was aghast. He had viewed Shepstone as an ally, albeit a condescending one, and when he heard the fixer was riding to Transvaal to take control the king's first action was to muster his iMpi on the border of the Disputed Territory and offer their support. He was prepared to go to war for Shepstone, and now it looked like he was coming to blows with him instead.

Sir Henry Bulwer, a career diplomat who had replaced Wolseley as lieutenant-governor of Natal, stepped into the bitter affair as a calm voice of caution. Bulwer rejected Shepstone's accounts of Zulu bloodlust and his spurious 'new evidence' of Boer ownership. Meeting with Cetshwayo, they agreed that Natal would form an independent Boundary Commission to rule on the matter definitively.

Playing the injured party, Shepstone told Frere on January 8, 1876, that, "I am satisfied that no permanent peace can be hoped for until Zulu power is broken up."

If Shepstone was hoping that the Natal Boundary Commission would do their bit for Queen and country, he had underestimated Bulwer's even-handed approach. Bulwer told his Transvaal counterpart frankly on January 16: "We are looking to different objects - I to the termination of this dispute by peaceful settlement, you to its termination by the overthrow of the Zulu Kingdom."

Publicly, Frere backed Bulwer's line but only as means to buy the war party time to build up their forces.

In February 1878 the rug was whipped out from under the feet of

The 'Ultimatum Tree' marks the location where the ultimatum was delivered. The sycamore fig itself is propagated from the original that stood on the site. WITSTINKHOUT CC BY-SA 3.0

confederation when Carnarvon resigned over the British government's aggressive posture towards Russia. His replacement Sir Michael Hicks Beach, known in Parliament as "Black Michael" for his bitter moods, was entirely fixated on the Russo-Ottoman War (1877-1878) and what it might mean for British interests in Asia and the eastern Mediterranean.

On the one hand, the appointment of Beach took confederation off the official agenda at the Colonial Office, but with his attention largely elsewhere the dominos that Shepstone and Frere had set in motions were already falling. Beach advised Frere in a letter of February 7 that "Shepstone would have to be discouraged from taking the opportunity to make war. The negotiations, through Bulwer, with Cetshwayo should be pushed on."

THE DOMINOES FALL

A colonial administrator of the old school who was happy to use the poor lines of communication with London to his advantage, Frere believed it was better to act unilaterally and receive the praise afterwards. He could manage without the support of the Secretary of State for the Colonies, but he could have done without the Boundary Commission ruling largely in favour of the Zulu.

The party from Natal had decided that the territory west of the Blood River should be administered by the Transvaal Colony by merit of them being long settled with the consent of the Zulu, but the vast majority of this thousand-square-mile prize was returned to Cetshwayo and its settler farms abandoned.

Shepstone's attempt to placate his Boer constituents had failed, and the casus belli for war with the Zulu had vanished with a single stroke of the pen. Shepstone's position

in the Transvaal was now so fragile that Frere had to have him recalled before the Afrikaners exploded into open revolt against the crown.

Just as one hawk flew for London, another flew in. Major General Frederic Thesiger - from October 1878 the 2nd Baron Chelmsford - was appointed commander-in-chief of British forces in southern Africa. Thesiger was the consummate Victorian gentleman officer who had been friends with Frere since their service together in India. He comported himself with great dignity and professionalism, was liked by his men, and shortly after his arrival he showed great pragmatism and sensitivity in commanding the mixed expeditionary force of British Army, colonial irregulars and African levies for the closing stages of the 9th Frontier War.

Thesiger believed in a clear division between military and policy. In his opinion, it was entirely for Frere to decide that the greatest threat to British interests was the Zulu, and then it was Thesiger's job to account for that threat.

He gathered all available military forces and marched for Natal. If the sudden deployment into his colony alarmed Bulwer, it was nothing compared to the memorandum that Thesiger handed him on August 24, 1878 entitled, 'Invasion of Zululand; or, Defence of the Natal and Transvaal from Invasion by the Zulu'. His battle plan - detailed in the following chapter - initially called for eight battalions, but at a push, Thesiger announced he could manage with fewer.

THE IMPOSSIBLE ULTIMATUM

Frere saw his opportunity in an incident that occurred earlier in July. Two wives of Chief Sihayo kaXongo of the Qungebe had fled across the Natal border seeking refuge

ABOVE · *Sir Henry Bartle Frere, painted in 1881 by George Reid and held by the National Portrait Gallery. Prior to the Anglo-Zulu War, Frere's highest office was as Governor of Bombay.*

THE DEADLY GRASP.

HALLO MYLADS „*THREE CHEERS FOR OLD ENGLAND* "

with their illicit lovers. They were pursued by a war party led by Sihayo's brother and sons, and the offenders were dragged back to Zululand and executed.

Not only this was a violation of Natal sovereignty, but it violated Shepstone's bogus coronation oaths about due process. Cetshwayo was slow to realise what Frere was driving at, and as Natal Mounted Police frequently crossed into Zululand in pursuit of fugitives he offered a £50 apology and considered the matter closed.

Another incident in September was promptly twisted to suit Frere's new reality. A surveyor and his friend had been interrogated by the Zulu while assessing a river for possible passage by wagons - an obvious overture for invasion. While Bulwer blamed Frere for provocation, Frere wrote to explaining the two men had been "seized and assaulted" by an armed Zulu party who crossed into Natal.

Cetshwayo confided in Bulwer: "I hear of troops arriving in Natal, that they are coming to attack the Zulus, and to seize me. What have I done wrong that I should be seized like a criminal? The English are my fathers, I do not wish to quarrel with them, but live as I have always done, at peace with them."

London by now was entirely focused on the Russian problem and the idea of a flare-up in southern Africa was an irritant. Begrudgingly, Beach authorised some - but not all - of the requested reinforcements, reasoning that it was an ample number for the defence of Natal if the threat of Zulu invasion were credible. He explained in a letter to the Prime Minister, Benjamin Disraeli, that he was "throwing as much cold water as possible upon [Frere's] evident expectation of a Zulu war."

By now Frere had fully slipped the leash. Although Beach had been unequivocal that he wasn't to incite conflict with Cetshwayo, as far as he was concerned his long-term aim was to bring about confederation and that could only be achieved by conquering Zululand.

With mixed, rambling references to the border violations, the settlement of the Disputed Territories and Cetshwayo's tyranny, Frere delivered an ultimatum of some 5,000 words to the king on December 11, 1878.

Amongst other things he demanded Sihayo's sons and brothers stand trial in Natal, 600 cattle as fine for various offenses, the disbanding of the Zulu iMpi and allowing its men to marry, and a British agent take up permanent residence and be present for all hearings involving a European. It represented the complete destruction of the Zulu Kingdom as an independent nation and shocked Cetshwayo to his core.

His choice was to either prepare for invasion or to allow himself to become little more than a client king at the indulgence of a white overseer, like so many before.

Cetshwayo pleaded for more time to discuss the implications with his council and to gather the cattle, but Frere refused - the king had to either meet the deadline or miss it, and by design he missed it.

The British would have their war.

Pretoria in 1877, taken by Swiss photographer Henri Ferdinand Gros, who was resident in Transvaal. This is believed to be the earliest photo of what was then a modest frontier town.

ABOVE · *A fanciful image of advancing British line infantry and scattering Zulu warriors from the cover of a piece of sheet music, The Zulu Expedition, Grand Military Fantasia.*

RIGHT · *Officers of the 24th Regiment of Foot pictured prior to the Anglo-Zulu War.*

THE RAGGED RED LINE

The British Army in Southern Africa

Chelmsford's army was a hybrid force. A curious mixture of hard-nosed and unruly colonial irregulars, untrained and poorly armed black levies, and seconded seamen moonlighting on land, it was based around a core of seven battalions of British infantry, but rather than a thin red line, it was a ragged red line patched with fetching dark blue, swashbuckling tan, and the exposed black skin of the African auxiliaries.

The deficiencies in command and control, his lack of regular cavalry, his insufficient artillery, and the expansive terrain he was expecting to pacify and conquer barely seemed to register. Chelmsford was a product of another world. After long service in India, he had caught the end of the 9th Frontier War and from it took the lesson that the enemy were likely to wage a guerrilla war and a dose of superior firepower would soon send the tribal rabble packing.

A Natal Border Agent was dispatched to gather intelligence and FB Fynney returned with a comprehensive portrait of the Zulu forces, their tactics and disposition. British artist Melton Prior recorded a meeting between Chelmsford and the leadership of the volunteer units during the closing stages of the 9th Frontier War, where the Boers advised the jingoistic general that as soon as they crossed into Zululand they had to form a laager at every stop.

"[Chelmsford] said 'Oh, British troops are all right; we do not need to laager - we have a different formation'."

His confirmation bias in full flow, Chelmsford failed to recognise the signs of a brutal warrior culture that thrived on massed charges, flanking manoeuvres, ambush and close quarter combat, and was expecting a repeat of the 9th Frontier War where a skirmish line of British soldiers would open fire with their breech-loading Martini-Henry rifles and deliver overwhelming victory.

"I am inclined to think that the first experience of the power of the Martini-Henrys will be such a surprise to the Zulus that they will not be formidable after the first effort," he wrote on November 23, 1878 to one of his twitchy subordinates.

Making a small force of 17,000 men and 20 guns even smaller, Chelmsford split his army into five columns that would march in five different directions from the Transvaal Colony and Natal Colony to close in on the Zulu royal kraal at Ulundi.

"Half measures do not answer with natives," he wrote to Shepstone. "They must be thoroughly crushed to make them believe in our superiority, and if I am called upon to conduct operations against them I shall strike to be in a position to show them how hopelessly inferior to us they are in fighting power, altho' numerically stronger."

THE TOMMY

Going into the Anglo-Zulu War, the British Army was an institution in transition - poised part-way between stiff stock collars and closely drilled ranks of the Peninsular Campaign and the fully professional, modern fighting force of 1914.

For the private soldier, the 12-year service of the mid-1800s had been replaced in 1870 by men signing up for contracts of (in the case of infantry) seven years full-time service and then five years with the reserves. Ostensibly this was to lower the costs of having an enormous standing army, while also providing for a part-time reserve force that could be mustered in times of need. It's the concept that the modern British Army is based on, and like the modern British Army it could find itself stretched woefully thin in times of crisis. Between 1860 and 1880, available manpower dropped by 23 per cent.

This was certainly the case at the end of 1878 and the beginning of 1879 when the streamlined British Army found that in addition to its existing commitments garrisoning the remote stretches of empire, it was being dragged into the 2nd Anglo-Afghan War, potential war with Russia over balance of power in the Balkans, and now Frere and Chelmsford's gunpoint nation building in southern Africa. This meant that an estimated 60 per cent of the men sent to the Cape ahead of the Anglo-Zulu War had only four months of service and the most basic of training. »»

The 24th Regiment of Foot on manoeuvres near Aldershot eight years prior to the Anglo-Zulu War, painted by Orlando Norie.

ARMS OF THE BRITISH ARMY

Martini-Henry Mark II

A British Army issue 1871-pattern Martini-Henry rifle held by the Armémuseum. THE SWEDISH ARMY MUSEUM

The earthly manifestation of Chelmsford's supreme overconfidence, the Martini-Henry entered service in 1871 and was replaced by the Mark II in 1874. A breech-loaded single-shot rifle, the Martini-Henry fired a heavy .450 lead bullet which flattened on impact to inflict horrific trauma, leaving gaping entry wounds and broken bones in its wake.

Sighted up to 1,450 yards, it was considered most effective at 350 yards, but prolonged use would reduce the rifle's effectiveness severely. The paper-clad cartridges were difficult to insert, the black powder quickly fouled the barrel causing rounds to become stuck, and the overheating of the barrel reduced accuracy and increased the already punishing recoil.

Socket Bayonet

Referred to as a 'lunger' by the men in the ranks for obvious reasons, the 22in socket bayonet was standard issue from 1876 and was inserted over the muzzle of the rifle with a locking ring to transform the firearm for close combat. The blade was triangular, with a flat surface facing upwards and the two bladed faces meeting at a downward edge.

An 1871-pattern sword bayonet with a cutting blade was used by infantry sergeants while men of the Naval Brigade used a cutlass bayonet.

The smaller artillery piece is an RML mountain gun, pictured here during the 2nd Anglo-Afghan War (1878-1880)

RML 7-pound Mountain Gun

The 7-pound RML (rifled muzzle-loader) Mark IV mountain gun had a maximum range of 3,200 yards and its snug size in contrast to the standard issue 9-pound field gun made it ideal for southern Africa.

Mounted on a specially designed narrow 'kaffrarian' carriage with oversized wheels five feet in diameter that redistributed its weight, the 7-pounder could be hauled by a team of six mules over the roughest roads.

.450 Adams Revolver

The first cartridge revolver approved for use by the British Army, the .450 Adams was adopted in 1865. A solid-frame, s[...] shot revolver, the .450 was only accurate within 25 yards. Relatively underpowered, it fell out of use not long aft[er] the Anglo-Zulu War.

A Mark III Adams Revolver issued in 1872. HARRYVC

The Cardwell Reforms of 1868-1874 also did away with the buying and selling of commissions in regiments, with a view to seeing privilege replaced by merit (although the class divide between officers and private soldiers remained insurmountable), removed corporal punishment such as flogging in times of peace, and created a new, standardised regimental system of at least two battalions. Regiments now recruited locally (previously recruits could be placed in any regiment), and one battalion would be based in Britain for training, while the other was stationed overseas. Each battalion was, in theory, made up of eight companies of 100 men (including officers).

The amount of kit an infantryman was expected to carry had been much reduced since the Crimean War two decades earlier from 68lbs to 57lbs. Combat critical equipment was contained within the 1871 Valise white leather webbing which distributed the weight evenly across the soldier's back and shoulders, with the rest of the infantryman's gear (including additional ammunition) stored in a wagon. The waist belt contained two pouches of 20 rounds on either side of the regimental buckle, a black leather 'expense pouch' of a further 30 rounds, and a bayonet frog at the rear. The shoulder straps supported a rolled great coat and mess tin, and a water bottle was usually slung over one shoulder and a canvas haversack over the other.

Red coats, however, remained in service. In the 1840s, British soldiers serving in India had moved to khaki (the Urdu word for dust, to reflect the improvised colouring of their white tropical dress) and halfway across the world, the army in Afghanistan marched over the mountains in khaki battle dress. However, in the equally punishing heat of Zululand they wore the traditional red tunic and it took until 1897 for khaki to formally replace scarlet for all men serving overseas.

One small mercy though, was that the tall shako hat - punishingly hot and heavy in India and Africa - had been replaced by the cork pith helmet during the 1850s, with the 1877 pattern (later referred to as the 'colonial pattern') helmet standard by 1879. With a wide brim sheltering the face and neck, the helmet was covered by white cloth (later dyed with tea for camouflage purposes) to reflect the heat, while ventilation around the hatband was provided by corrugated buckram or by eight cork wedges. The button or spiked (for officers) tip also had vents so that the warm air could rise through the crown.

THE OFFICERS

In many areas, progress travelled on a slow boat. The bulk of the senior officers gathered around Chelmsford were products of the old purchase system where wealth and family connections played a surer role in their careers than insight and ability. Connections remained vital at this level. With no standardised way of appointing staff officers to handle the operational side of command, Chelmsford enlisted like-minded men of means he knew and got on with.

Chelmsford's most trusted commanders were veterans of Britain's imperial wars who had served with him against the Xhosa, or had served at Crimea, cursing them with both a fatal confidence in the natural superiority of the British Army and its concentrated firepower, and an ▶▶▶

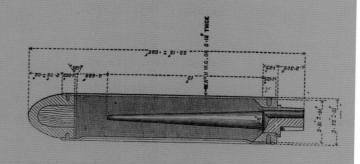

The first Webley revolver to see action with the British Army, it was the start of a 67-year love affair between the company and its biggest client. HMAAG CC BY-SA 3.0

Webley Royal Irish Constabulary Revolver

Especially popular with officers in the irregular colonial units, the 442 Webley was also considered underpowered but had an excellent rate of fire. It was the start of the British Army's long and fruitful relationship with the Webley that would take it through two World Wars and into the first decades of the Cold War.

Gatling Gun

The ancestor of the machine gun, the Gatling gun was a hand-cranked rotary cannon capable of delivering 600 rounds per minute. The rotating barrels prevented overheating and sped up the firing sequence, with rounds gravity fed from an ammo drum. The British Army had deployed a Gatling gun in the Ashanti Wars (1873-4) but had yet to fire it in battle.

Hales Rocket

Adopted by the British Army in 1867 and deployed on a collapsible three-pronged frame, the Hales rocket was stabilized in flight by a long stick and vents in the rear of the rolled steel rocket that spun it like a bullet over 1,200 yards.

The Naval Brigade brought two 24-pounder rockets to bear, which were fired from a tube (to prevent sparks flying wildly), while the British Army used the 9-pounder which was fired from a trough made from two long planks.

Easy to transport and capable of firing four rockets a minute, Hales rockets needed no specialist training to operate.

Primarily a psychological weapon, the Hales rocket was first used in the Crimean War with less than impressive results.

Two drum-fed Gatling guns in service in the Anglo-Afghan War (1878-1880)

Order of Battle

General Officer Commanding (GOC): Lieutenant General Lord Chelmsford, KCB

No.1 Column

Commander:
Colonel Pearson, 3rd Regiment of Foot

Infantry:
2/3rd Regiment of Foot
99th (Duke of Edinburgh's) Regiment
(6 companies)
Naval Brigade
2nd Regiment Natal Native Contingent
(2 battalions)

Cavalry:
No.2 Squadron Mounted Infantry
Natal Hussars
Durban Mounted Rifles
Alexandra Mounted Rifles
Stanger Mounted Rifles
Victoria Mounted Rifles

Support:
Royal Artillery (two 7-pounders)
No.2 Company Royal Engineers
No.2 Company Natal Native Pioneers

Total strength: 4,750 men,

No.3 Column

Commander:
Brevet Colonel Glyn, 24th Regiment of Foot

Infantry:
1/24th Regiment of Foot
2/24th Regiment of Foot
3rd Regiment Natal Native Contingent
(2 battalions)

Cavalry:
No.1 Squadron Mounted Infantry
Natal Mounted Police
Natal Carbineers
Newcastle Mounted Rifles
Buffalo Border Guard

Support:
Royal Artillery
No.5 Company Royal Engineers
No.1 Company Natal Native Pioneers

Total strength: 4,709 men

No.4 Column

Commander: Brevet Colonel Wood, VC,
CB, 90th (Perthshire Volunteers)
Light Infantry

Infantry:
90th (Perthshire Volunteers) Light Infantry
1/13th (1st Somersetshire)
(Prince Albert's Light Infantry) Regiment
of Foot

Cavalry:
Frontier Light Horse
Wood's Irregulars

Support:
Royal Artillery (six 7-pounders)

Total Strength: 1,565 men

No.2 Column (Reserve)

Commander: Lieutenant-Colonel
Durnford, Royal Engineers

Infantry:
1st Regiment Natal Native Contingent (3
battalions)

Cavalry:
Natal Native Horse (5 troop)

Support:
Rocket Battery
No.3 Company Natal Native Pioneers

Total Strength: 3,871 men

No.5 Column (Reserve)

Commander: Colonel Rowlands, VC, CB

Infantry:
80th Regiment of Foot (Staffordshire
Volunteers)

Cavalry:
Schutte's Corps
Transvaal Rangers
Border Horse
Eckersley's Contingent

Support:
Royal Artillery (six 7-pounders)

Total Strength: 2,278 men

---

attachment to discredited ways of waging war that was still in the process of being purged from the army's upper echelons.

The five columns were to be led by Brevet Colonel Henry Evelyn Wood, Brevet Colonel Richard Glyn, Colonel Charles Knight Pearson, and Colonel Hugh Rowlands. The black sheep of this family was Lieutenant Colonel Anthony Durnford, but more on him later.

Wood was the big beast and Chelmsford's most able commander, he had been awarded the Victoria Cross during the Indian Mutiny, and his experiences of Africa were shaped by the 3rd Anglo-Ashanti War (1873-4). Pearson and Glyn were both Crimea veterans who had been shipped out to southern Africa with 3rd Regiment of Foot (the Buffs) and 24th Regiment of Foot respectively.

Rowlands was another VC holder, in fact the first Welshman to receive the award, who had been seconded from 34th (Cumberland) Regiment of Foot for Special Service in southern Africa. This included a variety of roles, latterly as military Commandant of the Transvaal. An enormously resourceful and pragmatic officer.

Officers (as well as the enlisted men of the Royal Engineers and Royal Artillery)

preferred dark blue patrol jackets to scarlet tunics. Officers were responsible for buying their own sidearms and swords (primarily ceremonial, they were seldom used in anger). There was no standard issue revolver although the .450 Adams and .442 Webley RIC were most common.

COLONIAL IRREGULARS

One of the consequences of the Cardwell Reforms of 1868-1874 was the drawing down of British troops on overseas deployments. Spooked by a French war scare earlier in the century, Parliament had realised that the home islands were perilously vulnerable.

Though Cape Town, the capital of the Cape Colony, remained a garrison for the British Army, colonial authorities were also expected to recruit their own forces. Both Natal and Transvaal had militia at their disposal with wildly different compositions, character and levels of professionalism that were placed under Chelmsford's command.

Settler-formed mounted regiments - in the sense of having their own character and traditions, though they were well below regimental strength - were raised in different localities and were made up of part-time volunteers. The demands of settler life in Transvaal and Natal did give them some advantages; they were often excellent shots and horsemen, understood the terrain and conditions, and they equated service with their ownership of the land and the defence of their people. Transvaal regiments had a more overtly Boer character, but both colonies had something of that egalitarian commando ethos - men paid for their own uniforms and kit, and officers were elected.

This contribution was crowned by the Natal Mounted Police which was the only professional military in the colony.

ABOVE · *A late 19th century print showing the changing uniforms of the 24th Regiment of Foot, with the battle dress and sun helmets of the Anglo-Zulu War on the centre right next to the figures in khaki.*

A detachment of Natal Mounted Police with two Gatling guns. The photograph was taken after the Anglo-Zulu War.

ABOVE · *The various uniforms of the 3rd Regiment of Foot from 1572 to 1900, by which point they had become The Buffs (East Kent Regiment). The central figures represent the regiment in 1892, largely similar to how they would have appeared in 1879.*

ABOVE · *A sergeant in the Army Hospital Corps wearing the blue patrol jacket also favoured by infantry officers and all ranks of the Royal Engineers in the Anglo-Zulu War.*

A frontier gendarmerie of a few hundred men, the Natal Mounted Police recruited both white and black constables (to some protest locally) with a view to extending the fragile limits of colonial authority over a vast territory. Their contribution to the overall 17,000-strong force was limited, but they had at least a loyal, experienced, and highly professional officer cadre with which to exert influence over the strikingly individualistic colonial irregulars.

Cape Colony produced volunteer regiments too, but as the seat of British imperial power in southern Africa, they had a very different ethos from the hardy settler-farmers.

The Frontier Light Horse was an exceptionally professional body with a much-admired khaki uniform, they had fought with distinction in the 9th Frontier War and were led by a crop of senior officers seconded from the British Army.

Cape Colony also raised indigenous regiments to bring up the numbers, five troop of Natal Native Horse, three regiments of Natal Native Contingent and the 300-man Natal Native Pioneers, which caused alarm in Natal where white settlers were spread thinly and the idea of Africans with guns fuelled many a farmer's nightmares. The Governor of Natal fought tooth and nail against the arming of black auxiliaries in the territory, many

ABOVE · *Henry Evelyn Wood, pictured in 1916 in the rank of Field Marshal. Wood was appointed Knight Commander of the Order of the Bath following the Anglo-Zulu War and returned to Africa for the First Boer War (1880-1881), the Urabi Revolt (1879-1882) in Egypt, and the Mahdist War (1881–1899) in Sudan.*

of whom were Zulu or related tribes, but was eventually forced to relent when white reinforcements from Britain arrived in a dribble rather than a torrent.

Overall command of the native forces rested with Lieutenant Colonel Anthony William Durnford, Royal Engineers, who despite being a stranger to combat was an enthusiastic ally of confederation and the 'civilising' mission of empire. He commanded a great deal of respect from the black population of Natal, almost perfectly balanced by the ridicule from its white settlers. A typically eccentric colonial officer, Durnford had lost the use of his left arm in a skirmish that was described by many as a blunder and threatened to derail his entire career. To compensate for his patchy record in the field, Durnford was surrounded by experienced colonial soldiers, many of whom had experience leading black regiments and spoke Bantu languages.

Totalling 7,000 men across six battalions, the Natal Native Contingent was led by white officers and NCOs, and although each company

was recruited from a single tribe, the battalions were chaotically diverse. One man in every ten had a firearm, an older model breech-loading Snider rifle, while the rest made do with assegai and cow skin shields. Only a red bandana marked them out, frequently insufficiently, as friend rather than foe, and their role was to be limited to protecting the British supply wagons or chasing down retreating foes.

The Natal Native Horse were a far different beast and were personally trained by Durnford. Neatly uniformed in dusty yellow tunics, they were armed with Martini-Henry carbines and recruited from groups Durnford was sure would fight bitterly against the Zulu. As an engineer, he also took passionate interest in the

Natal Native Pioneers, who were considered the elite of the NNC, were given European-style uniforms and tools for the repairing of roads and the construction of defensive earthworks.

ARTILLERY AND SUPPORT
Though lacking regular cavalry, Chelmsford did have access to artillery. His forces were supported by No.5 Battery, Royal Artillery which fielded six 7-pounder rifled muzzle-loading guns, and a spectacular battery of three rocket launchers which fired a 9-pounder rocket from a collapsible metal frame. No.5 Battery had seen action in the 9th Frontier War and were placed under the command of Brevet Colonel Arthur Harness.

The 59th (2nd Nottinghamshire) Regiment of Foot during the 2nd Anglo-Afghan War (1880) wearing khaki battle dress. One of a series of military paintings by the Victorian artist Richard Simkin.

BRITISH BATTALIONS

1 and 2/24th Regiment of Foot

The 1st Battalion had been in Africa since 1875, serving in the 9th Frontier War, and contrary to the spirit of the Cardwell Reforms the 2nd joined them following overseas postings in the Far East. Though based in Brecon, they were previously designated the 24th (2nd Warwickshire) Regiment of Foot and most of the men were from the West Midlands.

1st Battalion was commanded by Brevet Colonel Richard Glyn and the 2nd by Brevet Lieutenant Colonel Wilson Black, a recent transfer to the regiment.

A watercolour caricature of an officer of the 24th Regiment of Foot in 1879.

2/3rd Regiment of Foot (The Buffs)

Based out of Canterbury Barracks from 1873, The Buffs already consisted of two battalions and so were largely unaffected by the Cardwell Reforms. The 1st Battalion were recently returned from active service in the Far East, so the 2nd Battalion sailed out under Colonel Charles Knight Pearson, a distinguished Crimean veteran but just as new as his men to the challenges of southern Africa.

An officer and infantryman of 3rd Regiment of Foot in their 1908 uniform by artist Harry Payne.

90th Regiment of Foot (Perthshire Volunteers)

After a spell garrisoning India and a long respite in Britain, the 90th Regiment of Foot (Perthshire Volunteers) (Light Infantry) were sent to Cape Colony in 1878 in time for the 9th Frontier War under the command of Brevet Colonel RM Rogers.

The 90th were linked to the 73rd (Perthshire) Regiment of Foot who were already serving in India, and so were the designated home battalion comprised mainly of soldiers who had yet to see battle or foreign climates.

The 1865 uniform of the 90th Regiment of Foot, illustrated by military artist Harry Payne.

80th Regiment of Foot (Staffordshire Volunteers)

An experienced colonial force, the 80th Regiment of Foot (Staffordshire Volunteers) arrived in Natal in 1877 under the command of Major Charles Tucker in time for the 9th Frontier War and were well acclimated to the environment and the demands of tribal warfare.

Partially untouched by the Cardwell Reforms, the 80th still consisted of a single battalion but was linked to the 38th (1st Staffordshire) Regiment of Foot, who served as the home battalion for the duration of the war.

The uniform of the South Staffordshire Regiment in 1900, by artist Harry Payne. The regiment was created by an amalgamation of the 80th Regiment of Foot with the 38th (1st Staffordshire) Regiment of Foot in 1881, two years after the Anglo-Zulu War.

99th (Duke of Edinburgh's) Regiment

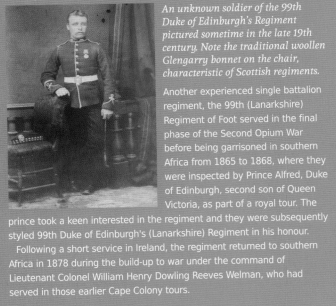

An unknown soldier of the 99th Duke of Edinburgh's Regiment pictured sometime in the late 19th century. Note the traditional woollen Glengarry bonnet on the chair, characteristic of Scottish regiments.

Another experienced single battalion regiment, the 99th (Lanarkshire) Regiment of Foot served in the final phase of the Second Opium War before being garrisoned in southern Africa from 1865 to 1868, where they were inspected by Prince Alfred, Duke of Edinburgh, second son of Queen Victoria, as part of a royal tour. The prince took a keen interested in the regiment and they were subsequently styled 99th Duke of Edinburgh's (Lanarkshire) Regiment in his honour.

Following a short service in Ireland, the regiment returned to southern Africa in 1878 during the build-up to war under the command of Lieutenant Colonel William Henry Dowling Reeves Welman, who had served in those earlier Cape Colony tours.

1/13th (1st Somersetshire) (Prince Albert's Light Infantry) Regiment of Foot

Officers of the 13th Regiment (DALI) in their 1880 uniforms by Orlando Norie.

1/13th Prince Albert's Light Infantry had been garrisoned at Gibraltar and then Malta from 1867, but soon got a taste of Africa's bloody tribal conflicts. Dispatched to southern Africa in 1874 under the command of Lieutenant Colonel Philip Edward Victor Gilbert - veteran of Crimea and the Indian Mutiny - for the 9th Frontier War, 1st Battalion were mounting operations against the BaPedi on the northeastern border of Transvaal when Chelmsford began to assemble his columns.

Artillery was also provided by the presence of the Royal Navy, and a Naval Brigade of seamen and Royal Marine Light Infantry contributed by HMS *Active*, HMS *Tenedos*, HMS *Shah* and HMS *Boadicea*. They brought with them small arms, rockets, Gatling guns and their dark blue sun helmets.

The Army Medical Staff attached medical officers at a regimental level, and the Army Hospital Corps supplied NCOs as orderlies, clerks, cooks and other support staff, and civilian nurses for day-to-day care in the field hospitals. Like regular army officers, the enlisted men of the Army Hospital Corps wore the blue patrol jacket.

Both AMS and AHC were subject to successive rolling reforms in an attempt to streamline the convoluted chain of command and division of responsibility. From 1873 they settled on a pragmatic solution that reflected the reality in the field: enlisted and civilian members of the Army Hospital Corps were under the command of the ranking medical officer at their station, usually an officer of the Army Medical Staff. ⟫

ABOVE · *A rural Natal Mounted Police station with both white European and black African officers, pictured in the late 19th century.*

The paramilitary Cape Mounted Rifles wearing their 1895 uniform, illustrated by Richard Simkins. In 1855 they were raised as the Frontier Armed and Mounted Police, changing their name to the Cape Mounted Riflemen in 1878 after an earlier disbanded regiment.

ABOVE · *Colonel Anthony William Durnford in 1870, just prior to receiving his posting for Cape Town. He had spent six years on garrison duty in England hungering for a colonial adventure.*

Less glamorous but vital, Lord Chelmsford was forced to wrestle with the demands of supplying the five columns of fighting men over hundreds of miles of forest, scrub, unpredictable rivers, and rock-strewn hills. Ox wagons and mule carts - along with the beasts to pull them and the teams to drive them - were purchased in huge numbers, with 16 oxen required to pull each heavy Voortrekker wagon over these unforgiving surfaces

a total of 27,000 oxen, 5,000 mules, and 2,500 wagons and carts were acquired.

These came under the control of the Commissariat and Transport Department, and the Army Service Corps, with responsibility for munitions provided by the Ordnance Store Department. The Army

ABOVE · *A member of the Army Medical Staff in dress uniform. The AMS existed between 1873 and 1898, before being amalgamated with the Army Hospital Corps to form the Royal Army Medical Corps.* WELLCOME COLLECTION CC BY 4.0

Service Corps had been created to do the grunt work in 1869 from the amalgamation of several logistic functions within other

units and served under officers from the C&TD and OSD. Also, in a support role were No.5 Company and No.2 Company Royal Engineers, who were split into detachments to serve where their skills were required.

Perhaps the greatest undertaking of Chelmsford's war planning, the supply trains would become his campaign's greatest vulnerability. It was the demands of keeping his forces supplied over hundreds of miles of uncertain roads that had formed the cornerstone of his strategy, reasoning that five trains would be less vulnerable and five columns less likely to be flanked.

By December 1878 he had revised his plan down to three columns. No.1 Column under Pearson would cross the Tugela River from Natal at Lower Drift and push 15 miles north to Eshowe; No.3 Column under Glyn would cross the Buffalo River from Natal at Rorke's Drift and march east; and No.4 Column under Wood would march from Transvaal through the Disputed Territory and through the north of Zululand.

Durnford's No.2 Column would move in support of No.1 Column and Rowland's No.5 Column was left to garrison the Transvaal Colony and protect No.4 Column's left flank. Chelmsford himself would march with the No.3 Column right into the heart of the slaughter.

One officer wrote: "We all thought and so did nearly everyone that they would come once at us and after getting most frightfully smashed, all organised resistance would be at an end." ◀◀◀

The 90th (Perthshire Volunteers) Light Infantry on parade in India, 1866.

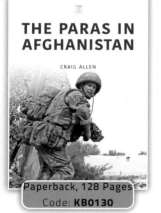

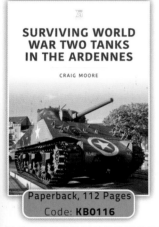
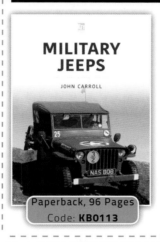

THE DAY OF THE DEAD MOON

The Battle of Isandlwana, January 22, 1879

The Battle of Isandlwana by Charles Edwin Fripp. As the Zulu rampage across the camp, the men of the 24th Regiment of Foot fight to the last man.

On January 11, 1879 4,700 men - at their heart, the 1st and 2nd Battalion of the British Army's 24th Regiment of Foot - crossed the Buffalo River at Rorke's Drift.

As commander of 1/24th, Brevet Colonel Richard Glyn was the nominal head of the column, but with Major-General Frederic Thesiger, 2nd Baron Chelmsford and his general staff in tow, the seasoned officer was pushed into a subordinate role.

The crossing took up most of the day and the following morning, with African levies wading through the chest-deep water and Europeans marching through the shallower drifts followed by the immense wagon train. The guns of the Royal Artillery kept careful watch from the opposite bank and a single company of 2/24th was left to garrison the crossing at Rorke's Drift. This unassuming mission station would soon become legendary.

Chelmsford had expected the crossing to be opposed by Chief Sihayo kaXongo and his 8,000 strong iMpi, but when battle failed to materialise four companies of 2/24th were dispatched along with a vanguard of Natal Native Contingent to take Sihayo's nearby kraal 'By the orders of the Great White Queen'. It was deserted save for a few women. Chelmsford ordered the village of mud and wood set aflame and the cattle driven back to friendly territory. Pushing on, they encountered one of Sihayo's sons and a small force of 60 warriors who were quickly slain.

This, thought Chelmsford, was evidence that either the Zulu lacked the guts to face the might of the British Empire, or they were holding back.

Calm Before the Storm

In fact, the Zulu were playing a long game and gathering in strength. King Cetshwayo kaMpande realised that No.3 Column was the most formidable and the one that needed to be broken. As his iMpi gathered

for war - some 40,000 warriors braying to 'wash their spears' in the blood of the enemy - he made clear the rules of engagement.

Despite Sir Henry Bartle Frere's claim that the Zulu King was "'an ignorant and bloodthirsty despot," Cetshwayo was determined to wage a war that left his people with a future and left him with room to negotiate once the British had been sufficiently bloodied. The local Zulu would be responsible for harassing No.1 and No.4 Column as they made their halting way through the unfriendly landscape, while the bulk of his army engaged Chelmsford's No.3 Column directly.

Cetshwayo ordered his men to march slowly so as not to tire themselves out, to avoid entrenched positions where British firepower would be the deciding factor, and to turn the enemy back but under no circumstances to cross the border into Natal.

The main Zulu army of 20,000 was placed under the command of the 70-year old Chief Ntshingwayo

"CHELMSFORD, MEANWHILE, WAS GRAPPLING WITH THE TATTERED INFRASTRUCTURE OF ZULULAND. THE TRACKS WERE TOUGH ENOUGH GOING FOR MEN ON FOOT, BUT THE RAINS HAD REDUCED THE LANDSCAPE TO A SWAMP THAT WOULD SLOW THE OX-DRAWN SUPPLY TRAIN TO A CRAWL."

was being helped no end by the eccentric Lieutenant Colonel Anthony Durnford. No.2 Column had been tasked with a supporting role and ordered to send two battalions of NNC to Sandspruit to watch out for Zulu incursions into Natal and, if necessary, quickly move northeast in support of No.3 Column. Instead, Durnford had acted on bogus reports of a counter-invasion and was bringing his whole force down to Middle Drift, half-way between Rorke's Drift and the ocean. Furious, Chelmsford ordered Durnford back into his position, threatening to relieve him of his command.

On January 15, Durnford was summoned to Rorke's Drift with his rocket battery, his elite Natal Native Horse and a battalion of NNC, leaving two poor quality infantry battalions behind to hold their position. Chelmsford was beginning to suspect that No.3 Column would likely face the toughest resistance and he needed another mounted regiment to recce the rolling hills. Durnford, for his part, was glad to be part of the action.

ABOVE LEFT · *Major John Dartnell leads the Natal Mounted Police and their ox-drawn supply train to the front on the eve of invasion.*

ABOVE · *The Irish adventurer and Natal Native Contingent commander Commandant George Hamilton-Browne, a veteran of frontier wars against the Māori in New Zealand and the Sioux in North America, offers a salute to the dead of the Battle of Isandlwana.*

Khoza as inDuna (headman or advisor). Medicines, a blend of herbs produced by the isAngoma (witch doctor), were burnt and sprinkled over the men as ritual purification and spiritual protection.

The spearhead were the unmarried men in their 20s and 30s, formed up into the uVe, iNgobamakhosi, uMcijo, uKhandempemvu ('The Sharp Pointed'), uMbonambi ('The Evil Seers'), uNokhenke, iMbube ('Lion'), uDudud, and iSangqu regiments. Older men in their 40s and 50s from the royal kraal made up the iNdluyengwe ('Leopard's Den'), uDloko, iNdlondo and uThulwana.

Thousands of young udibi boys, one for every four warriors at least, carried cooking

pots, shields, and sleeping mats. Amongst the regular duties of a scout, Zulus on horseback would drive cattle and sheep for the army to negate the need for a supply train.

Chelmsford, meanwhile, was grappling with the tattered infrastructure of Zululand. The tracks were tough enough going for men on foot, but the rains had reduced the landscape to a swamp that would slow the ox-drawn supply train to a crawl. Ditches were being dug by the pioneers either side of the track that passed for a road in the hope that it would drain sufficiently for the Royal Engineers to begin laying a 'corduroy' road of timber.

This week-long battle with the mud had put Chelmsford in a foul mood, and it

With the progress of No.3 Column far more torturous than hoped, Chelmsford decided to establish a camp at Isandlwana, 10 miles from Rorke's Drift, where they could consolidate. Brevet Colonel Evelyn Wood, whose No.4 Column was stationed at Bemba's Kop in the Disputed Territory between

Transvaal and Zululand, was too far away to actively support the main advance and so were encouraged to put pressure on northern kraals and send their cattle back across the border. Meanwhile, Colonel Charles Knight Pearson and No.1 Column would push from Lower Drift in the south up to Eshowe.

Step by step and kraal by kraal they would methodically round up the Zulu until their advance to the royal kraal at Ulundi was virtually unopposed. January was mid-harvest in southern Africa, and Chelmsford knew the Zulu lacked stores for a prolonged campaign.

"By this plan we will oblige Cetshwayo to keep his forces together," wrote Chelmsford, "when it shall suffer from want of food and become thoroughly discontented, or we shall oblige him to attack which will save us going to find him."

ISANDLWANA'S SHADOW

The eastern foot of Isandlwana Hill immediately provoked foreboding from the old hands, especially the colonials.

Major Francis Clery, Glyn's staff officer, chose the site. He was a former instructor at Sandhurst and had been foisted onto Glyn by Chelmsford despite his lack of combat experience. Inspector George Mansel of the Natal Mounted Police was leery in the extreme, protesting that they would be exposed to attack on all sides from the ridges and hills.

Chelmsford expected the Zulu to approach from the Mageni Valley, 》》)

TOP · *The Zulu charge at the British line. Spread too thinly to cover almost a mile of front, not even volley fire could halt the onslaught.*

ABOVE · *The bronze memorial to the Zulu dead was erected on the 120th anniversary of the battle in 1999. Its design was inspired by the isiqu, the Zulu necklace of valour with the claws echoing the chest of the formation and the thorns its horns.*

Though the choice of site troubled several senior officers, for most of the men Isandlwana seemed serene and no defensive precautions were taken.

The men were billeted across the track from left to right: 2/3rd Natal Native Corps; 1/3rd Natal Native Corps; 2/24th Regiment; No.5 Royal Artillery; the mix of colonial mounted units and their horses; and finally, the 1/24th Regiment. Behind them were the tents of the general headquarters and to the right of Isandlwana the hospital tents had been set up. Scattered chaotically behind the camp, wagons waited, ready to be sent back and forth from Rorke's Drift with supplies.

No wagons were laagered - the Boer practice of forming them up in a protective circle around the camp - and none of the boulders had been dragged from the rocky ground and heaped up to form cover. If the enemy advanced from the valley below, they would be spotted early and forced to charge uphill into a static line of Martini-Henry rifles.

Captain William Penn Symons, 2/24th wrote: "Everyone turned in early that night, not dreaming even of what was in store for the morrow. Indeed, so far, the invasion had been as autumn manoeuvres in pleasant but hot weather in England. Officers with permission went out alone shooting and prospecting miles from the camp, with no thought or risk of danger."

where a Zulu chief called Matshana had a kraal, and cut down objections with a snide word or two. A major of the 2/24th who offered a similar assessment to Chelmsford's secretary, Lieutenant Colonel John North Crealock, received an equally withering response. The coterie of staff officers, remarkable primarily for being old friends of their CO, had effectively formed an insulating bubble around their patron.

The camp faced Mageni Valley in the southeast, with high jagged hills on the left and a kopje, a smaller hill, on the right, and Isandlwana itself at their back. The plains around them were covered with tall grasses and creeping veins of donga - canyons formed from parched riverbeds - running north to south.

The ominous escarpment of Isandlwana. The name was said to derive from the isiZulu word for a cow's second stomach, due to the shape.

FALSE CONTACT

Having surveyed the hills a few miles distant of Isandlwana on January 20 and finding them disconcertingly quiet, Chelmsford formed up two parties for a more thorough search.

Just before dawn broke in the morning of January 21, he dispatched Commandant Rupert Lonsdale and both battalions of the Natal Native Corps to the Malakatas in the south. From there they would sweep up to rendezvous with Major John Dartnell of the Natal Mounted Police, who two hours later rode out to search the Nkhandhla Hills to the southeast. Accompanying Dartnell were over half the column's total cavalry and most of the NMP.

By four in the afternoon, Dartnell was finished. He was seven miles from the camp, and Lonsdale - his white NCOs exhausted and irritated from scrambling around the thorny hillside on foot - led his men up to join him, where Dartnell had decided to spend the night. Their search had revealed more empty kraals where only a few women remained to tend the cattle and a handful of Zulu deserters who were tortured until they revealed they left the iMpi at Isipezi Mountain to the east.

The intelligence was sent back to Chelmsford and largely ignored as it didn't fit with the direction of his expected assault, but then Dartnell's outriders spotted something that did. A troop of Natal Mounted Police reported several hundred Zulus in the Magogo Hills beyond the Nkhandhla. The major sent a rider to Isandlwana for permission to strike at first light. He received it, along with (some, but not enough) rations and blankets for the bivouacking men.

Mutiny was brewing among the white ranks of the NNC. Made up of drunkards, thieves and other lowlives too disreputable to serve in the colonial regiments, they had no stomach for a fight - literally, as it would be their second day without rations. Two lieutenants, several NCOs and some of their black soldiers simply walked back to Isandlwana when Lonsdale wasn't looking.

The ever-vigilant Lieutenant Archibald Milne, Chelmsford's Royal Navy aide-de-camp, had spotted 14 Zulu horsemen keeping watch from a plateau four miles to the northeast. The general made a note to investigate the next day but didn't follow it up once events elsewhere began to muzzle his situational awareness.

As night fell, Dartnell noticed more Zulu slipping over the ridge three miles to the east and into the Magogo foothills. The force now numbered as many as 2,000 and what looked like an opportunity for an easy triumph had faded with the light. Darkness slowing the messenger to a walking pace, it wasn't until the following morning that Chelmsford learned what had shattered Dartnell's bravado. Despite reports of Zulu scouts to the northeast and the deserters' claims of leaving their iMpi at Isipezi, the Zulu army seemed to be exactly where Chelmsford had expected to find it.

He took Glyn and six companies of 2/24th to reinforce Dartnell, minus G Company which was already on picket duty with Lieutenant Charles d'Aguilar Pope. Five companies of 1/24th under Brevet Lieutenant-Colonel Henry Pulleine remained at Isandlwana, supported by Pope's company of 2/24th. A capable manager but lacking in leadership, Pulleine was placed in command and given relatively simple orders to remain in a defensive posture, keep his infantry in a line and keep the ammunition wagon loaded in case Chelmsford called for it.

Chelmsford also brought up four of the Royal Artillery's six guns under Major Arthur Harness, with the Natal Native Pioneers to aid their passage. This left a battery of two 7-pounders at camp. Approximately 600 black auxiliaries also remained, and roughly 100 colonial cavalry. Durnford was ordered to move his expeditionary force up from Rorke's Drift to reinforce Isandlwana and leave the crossing in the capable hands of a company of 2/24th, plus 300 Bantu reserves.

Reaching Dartnell at six in the morning, Chelmsford found the irregulars had spent a restless night watching the Zulu campfires on Magogo, the cold, hungry and weary white officers struggling to keep their cold, hungry and weary African levies from bolting at every creak of the trees. As light broke the enemy had all but vanished with only a few stragglers spotted darting across the distant hills.

Chelmsford spent the rest of the morning dragging his men up and down the dongas and hills trying to find his Zulu quarry like a country squire on a hunt.

THE GATHERING STORM

The Zulu army had spent the night hidden in the canyon of Ngwebeni Valley to the northeast.

The day before they had arrived at Isipezi and using Chief Matshana's knowledge of the local area, a diversionary force had been sent south to Magogo to present the British with a tempting target. The warriors lit fires and kept them burning through the night while peeling off in small groups to rejoin the main force. Meanwhile, Ntshingwayo had led the army north, where they could shelter northeast of the Nqutu Plateau.

If anything, the plan had worked too well. January 22 was a day sacred to the Zulu. Marked by a waning 'dead' moon, it was a day when no harvest was to be gathered nor battles be fought, but with Chelmsford leading half of the British force on a search of the undulating hills and riverbeds to the south where Matshana's iMpi remained to keep him busy, the opportunity to strike at the sleepy row of British tents was too tempting.

A few hours after Chelmsford's departure, two scouts from the Natal Carbineers six miles east of the camp caught sight of the Zulu. Galloping back to Isandlwana, they were met by Lieutenant Neville Coghill of the 1/24th Regiment and he took the message to Lieutenant Colonel

A panoramic photograph of the Isandlwana battlefield as it appears today. BIZCALLERS CC BY-SA 3.0

"SAVE THE COLOURS!"

The Anglo-Zulu War was one of the last conflicts where regiments of the British Army marched into battle with their colours.

Each regiment typically carried two gold-edged banners: the sovereign's colours, which was the union flag with a crown and the regiment's name, and the regimental colours, which was the colour of the regiment's uniform facings and was adorned by the regimental crest and battle honours. The colours were a source of pride for the enlisted men and they were traditionally used to reorganise broken lines in the heat of battle.

During the retreat from Isandlwana, Lieutenant Teignmouth Melvill was seen riding with the Queen's colours in one hand, accompanied by Lieutenant Neville Coghill. Coghill was seen leaving the field first, where after his horse was wounded he encountered the retreating Melvill. The two battled on through the press of panicked bodies and Zulu pursuers, eventually perishing trying to cross the Buffalo River.

A story that circulated after the battle claimed that Brevet Lieutenant Colonel Pulleine had given Melvill the colours and ordered him out of the camp, and that the two had died defending them. The Victorian public, desperate for some hope to cling to in the aftermath of the catastrophe latched onto this symbol of British military honour and duty, and both men were awarded the Victoria Cross posthumously.

Lieutenants Coghill and Melvill make their heroic dash for safety in 'Saving the Queen's Colours', by Alphonse de Neuville.
© NAIRN MUSEUM

Modern historians have been more sceptical. Pulleine virtually disappeared from the battle once the British lines contracted. Many officers - including Durnford - looked in vain for the camp's commander, so it seems unlikely that Melvill encountered him without anyone noticing.

It's also unlikely Melvill grabbed the colours with the intention of rallying the regiment into a defiant last stand, as others have claimed. At the time of the young officer's

Chelmsford discovers the bodies of Lieutenants Coghill and Melvill, cradling the colours of the 1/24th Regiment of Foot, in 'Last Sleep of the Brave', a romanticised portrait by Alphonse de Neuville. © NAIRN MUSEUM

death they were still cased in leather, and as we've discovered there were plenty of opportunities for a blaze of glory. Instead, it's been suggested that Melvill took the colours and fled with them to provide a heroic alibi for his retreat at a time when so many others were standing firm. It's worth noting that Melvill and Coghill are the only officers of the 24th Regiment known to have left the battlefield.

Pulleine. Not entirely sure what he was dealing with, Pulleine sent a rider to inform the general and then ordered the camp stand to.

He had almost 1,600 men under his command, but only 1,241 were combat troops and of that number only approximately 600 were professional line infantry of the British Army. Already, Pulleine was indecisive and ordered the support staff - the cooks, farriers, orderlies and so on – to return to their potato peeling.

Reports from the scouts kept coming in a chaotic and contradictory flurry, and confronted with a situation he couldn't understand, Pulleine settled for doing nothing. The Buffalo Border Guard told one officer, possibly Coghill, that there were between 25,000 and 30,000 Zulus on the move. It was an exaggeration, but as a scale of threat facing the British, it wasn't far off the 20,000 warriors Ntshingwayo led into the area.

Shortly after 10am, Lieutenant Colonel Durnford arrived followed by five troop of elite Natal Native Horse, all from the same tribe and called Zikali's Horse, two companies of Natal Native Contingent, and a mule-drawn rocket battery - 526 men in all. Seeing distant Zulu, he immediately sent six of his own scouts to discern their disposition and direction. Then he let himself into the tent that served as general headquarters.

Durnford was undisputedly the ranking officer, he was a full lieutenant colonel whereas Pulleine's rank was brevet, meaning he had been promoted in the field but it wasn't necessarily permanent. On the other hand, Pulleine had been placed unambiguously in charge of the camp, it was his regiment about to fight on the line, while Durnford was a maverick engineer commanding a column of 'natives'.

The exact exchange between the two most senior officers in the camp is unconfirmed, but one witness recalled that Pulleine gave Durnford a situation report and then repeated several times that he had been ordered to defend the camp. It's entirely possible that each man left the conversation with a different outcome in their mind: Pulleine would defend Isandlwana as he had been tasked and in the precise way he had been instructed to do it, and Durnford would march to the beat of his own drum.

That at least is how they went about their business. When Durnford's scout returned reporting that the Zulu now appeared to be in retreat, Durnford decided to give chase and stop them creeping up behind Chelmsford's party. He asked Pulleine for two companies of 2/24th and their characteristic refrain started up again. Pulleine said the purpose of the 2/24th was to defend the camp, so Durnford gathered up some of the colonial cavalry to join his own and set off in pursuit across the long swaying grass.

After four miles a scout from the Natal Carbineers frantically caught up with them. It was another feint to draw yet more defenders away from the prize.

CAUGHT IN THE HORNS

While the enemy galloped back and forth across the rolling waves of grass, Ntshingwayo had been carefully moving unit after unit of his warriors closer and closer to Isandlwana, using the shelter of the dongas, hills and slopes to maintain surprise. He was mounting the traditional Zulu offensive formation across miles of terrain: The Horns of the Buffalo, its left and right horns set to gore the thinly protected flanks of the British camp, while its chest drew their fire on the southeastern approach.

Sometime around noon, Captain George Shepstone (son of Sir Theophilus Shepstone) and a troop of Zikali's Horse had ridden up to the Nqutu Plateau. Carefully making their way up the escarpment, they watched some Zulu driving a herd of cattle until they dropped out of sight behind a ridge. Giving chase, they wheeled about in horror.

"We saw Zulus, like ants, in front of us in perfect order, quiet as mice and stretched across in an even line," recalled Acting Commissariat Officer James Hamer. "We estimated those we saw at 12,000."

The Zulu opened fire and then charged as Zikali's Horse beat a fighting retreat, firing their carbines from the saddle while

Shepstone and Hamer raced to warn Pulleine. The Natal Native Contingent broke and fled before the right horn of the Zulu army, leaving their commanding officer screaming curses at their backs. Durnford turned to the sound of carbines cracking to the north, the left horn broke from cover and charged the disorientated irregulars and Durnford's men too began a fighting retreat towards the camp.

The rocket battery was hastening towards the sounds of battle, directed by a Natal Carbineer, and fired its unpredictable payload at movement on the crest of Nqutu Plateau. A single useless rocket burst against the rocks before the Zulu swept down, opening fire on the artillerymen and killing four. The mules bolted and the NNC escort followed, and the remaining

BELOW · *The Last of the 24th by Richard Thomas Moynan depicts one of the soldiers of C Company, who was said to have made his stand in a cave. When the battlefield was surveyed after the war, a cave was found filled with spent cases and a skeleton lay directly beneath it where its occupant had been dragged into the sunlight.*

BELOW LEFT · *The ill-fated Brevet Lieutenant Colonel Henry Pulleine, pictured in civilian clothes sometime before 1879.*

soldiers were only saved by the sudden appearance of the retreating Durnford and two companies of cavalry.

While Durnford led his mean to a nearby donga where they could take up a defensive posture, Pulleine's bizarre behaviour continued. He ordered a company of 1/24th up to provide support, and then dismissed the rest, telling them to go and get some lunch.

Just as Shepstone and Hamer burst into the GHQ to deliver their urgent warning, they were interrupted by a messenger from Chelmsford. He instructed Pulleine to begin packing up the camp and move up to join them. The acting CO was frozen. As gently and firmly as he could Shepstone said: "I'm not an alarmist, sir, but the Zulus are in such black masses over there, such long black lines, that you will have to give us all the assistance you can. They are now fast driving our men this way."

Pulleine elected to stretch his small force even thinner. Men were sent up in batches to support Durnford's position, while the rest of the 24th were ordered to form a wide perimeter - 600 men covering nearly a mile of frontline - in accordance with the doctrine that a skirmish line of disciplined British infantry armed with repeating rifles would be enough to see off the Zulu. Behind them, Pulleine placed his rump of remaining colonial cavalry and the two guns of the Royal Artillery were stationed forward of the left flank to cover the approach. What was left of the Natal Native Contingent was to defend the rear, but they soon broke and ran for home.

The right horn exposed by Shepstone was now outflanking the left of the British line, sweeping over the hills to the north of the camp. The battered band he had led up Nqutu Plateau and then back down were desperately forming up with C Company, 1/24th to face this new danger, and steeled by volley fire from the redcoats they briefly forced the uNokhenke regiment back over the ridge. It was valiant, but it wouldn't save Isandlwana from slaughter.

Military catastrophe has only one hierarchy of blame and it starts at the top. No senior officer involved in the Battle of Isandlwana is above criticism for their role in how the day unfolded, but it would be the survivors who might lose their careers and reputations. The dead could no longer tell their story, so the living told it for them.

In the aftermath of the Anglo-Zulu War, Queen Victoria recorded in her diary a meeting with Lord Chelmsford, who told her that Durnford had disobeyed orders to take command of the camp - no such orders were given - and had abandoned it by leading the cavalry off into the plains.

He also claimed Durnford had not sent a message making clear the danger Isandlwana was in - hiding the fact that he had received plenty of messages to that effect behind the lie that Durnford was in command.

A bizarre drama stirred up by an officer with an axe to grind continued to drag Durnford's name through the dirt for decades. Differing accounts surrounding the discovery of the lieutenant general's body alternately suggested he was found without a coat - and therefore no written orders exonerating him - or that he was found with a coat, and his personal effects had been removed - and therefore the written orders hidden.

It wasn't until the order book of Chelmsford's secretary was examined in the 1960s that it became clear that Durnford was ordered to 'support' the men at Isandlwana, and not to take command of them as the general had claimed.

INTO THE STORM

Brevet Major Stuart Smith flung shell after shell from his two mountain guns uselessly into the oncoming chest of the Zulu army. "The Zulus soon split up into a large mass of skirmishers that extended around the camp as far as we could see," described Lieutenant Henry Curling, Royal Artillery. "We could get no idea of numbers, but the hills were black with them."

For now, at least, the chest and the left horn were being kept at bay. Urged on by Durnford who galloped up and down the line as if he were presiding over a shooting range at a fairground, the 150-odd men protected by the earth walls of the donga fired round after round into the oncoming storm.

Though much attention has been paid to the cantankerous Quartermaster Edward Bloomfield who refused to issue ammunition to men not of his regiment, the major impediment to resupplying the men in the firing line was their rate of fire and their distance from the camp itself.

Lieutenant Horace Smith-Dorrien, a transport officer for the Royal Artillery and so at a loose end in a firefight "had collected camp stragglers such as artillerymen in charge of spare horses, officers' servants, sick etc, and had taken them to the ammunition boxes, where we broke them open as fast as we could, and kept sending out the packets to the firing line."

Despite the best efforts of Smith-Dorrien, Durnford was forced to pull his mounted force from the donga as man by man they exhausted their last cartridge. The left horn had tacked to the south to loop around their withering fire, and they were in danger of being cut off - out of ammo and out of luck, waiting in a ditch to die.

As the retreating men flooded into the camp, Pulleine ordered the perimeter pulled back to keep from being outflanked on both sides. Once the 7-pounders ceased firing, the Zulu charged the battery. The guns themselves were pulled crashing and bouncing back to safety, but the artillerymen who failed to leap onto the carriage as it sped off were cut down in flight.

A British soldier in full retreat, swaddled in pouches, his water flask and bayonet swinging as he runs is no match for an unencumbered Zulu. With the contraction of the British line, the iMpi were darting among them, their blades flashing in the sun as they cut down the retreating infantry like red dominos. The battle for the camp was over, it was now a desperate fight for survival.

"In a moment, all was disorder and few of the men had time to fix bayonets before the enemy was among them using their assegais with fearful effect," said transport officer Captain Edward Essex. "I heard a few officers calling for their men to be steady; but the retreat became in a few seconds general, and in a direction towards the road to Rorke's Drift. Before however, we gained the neck towards Isandlwana Hill, the enemy had arrived in that portion of the field also, and the large circle had now closed in on us."

TOO LITTLE, TOO LATE

At 9.30 that morning, a message on light blue notepaper was handed to Chelmsford from a dispatch rider: "Report just come in that the Zulus are advancing in force from left front of camp."

Chelmsford was perplexed, but not overly concerned. Pulleine hadn't requested support and there was no hint of urgency in the message. He reasoned that the Zulu were most likely an advance party, and by the time the messenger arrived his letter was two hours old, and it would take Chelmsford another three hours to move his force back to camp only to bring them all 12 miles back out again to form a new camp at Mangeni Falls.

The coerced confession from the Zulu deserters and the reports of mounted scouts to the northeast played on his mind though, and Chelmsford sent his ADC, Lieutenant Milne, to find some high ground from where he could observe Isandlwana. Through the distant haze of heat, he made out what looked like 500 Zulu in retreat. Everything looked under control.

In a contrast so surreal it would be laughable were men not fighting for their lives, Chelmsford took breakfast. Returning with his exhausted 1/3rd Natal Native Contingent from scrapping with Matshana's warriors, Commandant George Hamilton-Browne recalled his disbelief: "I shall never forget the sight of the peaceful picnic. Here were the staff quietly breakfasting and the whole column scattered across the country!"

Hamilton-Browne turned down the general's generous offer of a place at the table. His men hadn't been properly provisioned, and he would suffer with them. For their pains, they were ordered back to Isandlwana to help take down the camp.

Just before midday, Chelmsford heard the guns of Isandlwana open fire. His officers ran up a slope to level their eyeglasses in the direction of the camp where they saw shells land and then the artillery suddenly fell silent. Rather than take this as an ill omen, Chelmsford thought it a sign that whatever Zulu offensive had struck Isandlwana had been beaten back.

On the slope of a nearby hill where the artillery had formed up, Major Harness listened to the distant 7-pounders with a growing sense of unease. A few hours earlier, he watched Hamilton-Browne and the 1/3rd NNC wearily set off to Isandlwana, and now he watched them turn back. One of the officers peeled away from the line of black infantry and galloped towards them. Harness sent his bugler on horseback to intercept.

The message turned the major's blood to ice: "For God's sake come back with all your men; the camp is surrounded and [will] be taken unless helped."

Harness began turning his guns and started back for Isandlwana. Noticing the flurry of activity, an officer from Chelmsford's staff rode up to investigate. Major Matthew William Gosset shared the general's view that the matter would be settled by the time they got there and that Isandlwana could defend itself. He accused Harness of 'insubordination' and to his credit the artilleryman stood firm, demanding confirmation from the general on the matter.

Gosset had guessed right. Chelmsford brushed the message aside and ordered Harness down to Mageni Falls. The 7-pounders were turned again, as if unable to stand the shame.

The Circle Closes

As a press of bodies pushed towards Rorke's Drift road between Isandlwana and the kopje, survivors remember seeing Lieutenant Colonel Durnford and a company of the 24th Regiment desperately fighting on to keep the escape route open. Others fought gallantly too to resist a massacre of the retreating British, using their rifles like clubs when the last round was spent.

Captain George Shepstone had rallied some of the Natal Native Contingent to hold back the right horn, and Captain Reginald Younghusband of C Company, 1/24th had climbed up the escarpment with 67 men to a rock shelf and died hard. The last redcoat to fall was said to be a man of C Company, who crawled into a cave nearby and kept his attackers at bay until a volley of Zulu fire killed him.

The clattering gun carriages of the Royal Artillery arrived to find the pass choked by the urgent throng and being squeezed by the horns of the Zulu. The wheels became stuck, so the guns were cut loose, and the officers rode on without them. Cavalry had the best

chance of escape, though they were being forced away from the road and across open ground strewn with rocks where they found themselves in another trap.

A deep donga with a stream of shallow water blocked their path, forcing the retreat to descend into it and follow its twisting concourse towards the Buffalo River and the safety of Natal. All the while, above them Zulus taunted their prey with war cries, bullets and spears. One survivor, interpreter James Brickhill, recalled the nightmarish scene:

"Our way was already strewn with shields, assegais, blankets, hats, clothing of all descriptions, guns, ammunition belts, saddles (which horses had managed to kick off), revolvers, and I do not know what. Whilst our stampede was composed of mules, with and without pack saddles, oxen, horses in all stages of equipment and fleeing men all strangely intermingled - man and beast, apparently all infected with the danger that surrounded us. One riderless horse that ran up alongside of me I caught and gave to a poor soldier, who was struggling along on foot, but he had scarcely mounted before he was knocked down by a Zulu bullet."

At the end of the donga the steep descent towards the river and safety was perilous and could only be done in single file. A bottleneck formed and as the Zulu closed

in, men flung themselves wildly into the water below. Of the force of over 1,700 men that held Isandlwana on the morning of January 22, only 55 white and 350 black survivors made it to the banks of Natal across what became known as Fugitives' Drift.

How, when and where Brevet Lieutenant Colonel Pulleine was killed is still unknown.

The British dead were disembowelled where they lay to release their spirits and prevent them poisoning their killers. Over a thousand rifles were taken and 250,000 rounds of ammunition, before the approach of Chelmsford's force just before sunset sent the Zulu back into the hills.

The toll for the Zulu was enormous too, and anywhere between 1,000 and 3,000 warriors had fallen in the taking of Isandlwana. When the news reached the king, Cetshwayo exclaimed: "An assegai has been thrust into the belly of the nation. There are not enough tears to mourn for the dead."

It's been said that Chelmsford delayed his return until last light so that he wouldn't have to gaze upon the full scale of the carnage, but by all accounts, the general was distraught and set off as soon as he became aware of the scale of the disaster.

As the darkness set in, the British relief column spent a cold and anxious night in the ruins of Isandlwana, surrounded by the flickering campfires of the Zulu in the hills and the distant rattle of gunfire over Rorke's Drift. ◁◁

One of the many cairns at the site of the battle marks a mass grave of the British fallen.

"AN ASSEGAI HAS BEEN THRUST INTO THE BELLY OF THE NATION. THERE ARE NOT ENOUGH TEARS TO MOURN FOR THE DEAD."

THE COMPANY OF HEROES

The Battle of Rorke's Drift, January 22-23, 1879

On January 17, 1879 Lieutenant John Rouse Merriott Chard, Royal Engineers arrived at the gleaming white canvas tent city outside Rorke's Drift, it stretched out on a gentle slope that still bears the name Matosheni ('The Hill of the Soldiers').

The mule-drawn wagons of No.5 Engineer Company were delayed by the heavy rain in the run up to invasion, their wheels dragging in the mud as they made their frustrating crawl to the Natal border. By the time they caught up with the rest of No.3 Column, Lord Chelmsford's force was part-way through its move up to the new camp in the shadow of Isandlwana.

With the immense undertaking of moving an entire army well underway, Chard probably didn't have that much time to fully grasp the context of his situation. Placed in charge of the pontoon bridge across the Buffalo River, he immediately set to work with his team of sappers to patch up the wear and tear along this vital artery of the British advance.

By January 21, Matosheni was nearly deserted with only the recently arrived Lieutenant Colonel Anthony Durnford and his 500-strong band of Natal Native Horse and Natal Native Contingent proof of a once thriving camp. Durnford had been ordered up to Isandlwana too and his departure would leave the bridge totally unprotected, too far from the Rorke's Drift mission to take shelter under its guns and its garrison is too small to be extended out to the banks of the Buffalo River.

At this stage, in what would become the Battle of Rorke's Drift, Chard's entire world is that bridge. Not only is it now vulnerable to attack, but so is he and army doctrine asserts that in the field an engineer should be protected by infantry. On the black morning of January 22, Chard heads up the road to Isandlwana to clarify his orders.

Chard arrives to discover that Chelmsford and half of the force have already moved on, sallying out to hunt the iMpi in the hills to the southeast. From Isandlwana, Zulu are visible on the hills, but Chard is assured that the defence of the bridge has

The Defence of Rorke's Drift by Alphonse de Neuville. This famous painting includes a number of individuals involved in the battle, from left to right: Assistant Commissary Walter Dunne (in blue, moving a biscuit box), Private Henry Hook (in blue, carrying a man on his back) Private Frederick Hitch (with his head bandaged, behind Bromhead), Lieutenant Gonville Bromhead (standing in the middle of the compound pointing), Surgeon James Reynolds (attending to Dalton's wound with his terrier), Acting Assistant Commissary James Dalton (sitting in the foreground with a shoulder wound), Chaplain George Smith (the bearded man with his hand in his ammunition sack), Corporal Ferdinand Schiess (in the tan uniform, stabbing a Zulu with his bayonet), Lieutenant John Chard (bareheaded with the grey breeches and rifle).

LEFT · *A map showing the site of the battle in relation to Isandlwana and Isipezi, where Chelmsford's force was heading on January 22, 1879.*

BELOW · *How the mission station appeared prior to the outbreak of the Anglo-Zulu War, with the chapel to the left and the house on the right, and Oscarberg looming behind.*

been accounted for by the general staff - a company of 1/24th Regiment of Foot under Captain Thomas Rainforth have been called up from Helpmekaar in Natal.

On his way back to the drift, Chard passed Durnford heading in the other direction and quickly updated him on the Zulu threat to the camp. One engineer then rode towards his death, and the other rode towards glory.

TRADERS, MISSIONARIES AND SOLDIERS

At the end of the war, King Cetshwayo kaMpande was said to have uttered: "First comes the trader, then the missionary, then the red soldier." It's most likely apocryphal, but it neatly sums up the story of Rorke's Drift.

Rorke's Drift had been settled as a farm in 1849 by an Irishman called James Rorke. The farmhouse on the rocky ledge soon grew to become a trading post and the track crossing the river through the shallow drift, or ford, grew into a rough-hewn road.

Popular both sides of the Buffalo, the Zulu called the station kwaJimu ('Jim's Place'). Rorke built himself a single-storey farmhouse with a thatched roof and 11 rooms, five of which could only be accessed from the outside, so they could be rented out to lodgers. Rorke built a small store of the same simple brick and thatch design. Both buildings had wide verandas.

Rorke passed away in 1875 and in 1878 his property was acquired by the Norwegian Missionary Society with a view for using it as a base from which to take the word of God to Zululand. Reverend Otto Witt, a missionary from Sweden, took up residence and turned the store into a chapel. He also renamed the hill behind the station Oscarberg in honour of the King of Norway and Sweden, Oscar II (1872–1907). The wooden cattle kraal northeast of the chapel was replaced by a more robust stone walled one. There was also a smaller stone kraal directly adjoining the chapel

Despite his depiction in the 1964 film, *Zulu*, Otto Witt wasn't a gimlet-eyed hysteric cursing the British Army and predicting doom (though he did later sue them successfully for destruction of property). On the outbreak of the Anglo-Zulu War, he made the mission available to the British and was paid rent for his trouble. Most missionaries were supportive of the British invasion as their evangelism had yielded little interest from the Zulu, and they saw taking Christianity to the 'savages' to be part of the civilising mission of empire.

Witt moved his family away from the border in January 1879 and joined them himself immediately prior to the attack.

The army's Commissariat and Transport Department had transformed the chapel back into a storeroom, filled with bags of mealie (local grain), ammunition and other supplies required for No.3 Column. The house, meanwhile, had been taken over by

ABOVE · *An etching of Lieutenant Gonville Bromhead in civilian attire. His father was Sir Edmund de Gonville Bromhead, 3rd Baronet, a veteran of the Battle of Waterloo.*

the Army Medical Department and was filled with the column's 35 miscellaneous wounded, a few had picked up scrapes clearing Chief Sihayo's kraal but most were fighting off dysentery, trench foot and other

Tiny against Oscarberg and the distant Buffalo River, Rorke's Drift is dwarfed by the landscape in this photograph.

unglamorous realities of colonial warfare.

Assistant Commissary Walter Dunne was in charge of the stores, while the field hospital was the domain of Surgeon James Henry Reynolds, his three staff from the Army Hospital Corps, and his terrier, Dick. Dunne was joined by the impressive and soon to be heroic figure of Acting Assistant Commissary James Langley Dalton.

One of the men most ill-served by *Zulu*, rather than a genteel battle-shy administrator, Dalton had been in uniform since the age of 17 and worked his way up through the ranks to corporal and then staff sergeant. He had been discharged in 1871 and emigrated to southern Africa when the war brought a new opportunity to serve. Though technically a civilian, the 44-year old was the most experienced man stationed at the mission.

Brevet Major Henry Spalding, 104th Regiment of Foot, was the commanding officer of Rorke's Drift. A member of Chelmsford's staff in charge of communication and supplies, Spalding had served in the Indian Mutiny but otherwise remains a fairly anonymous figure. The striking figure of Chaplain George Smith was also present.

Smith had been working as a missionary in Africa since 1870.

Protecting Rorke's Drift were B Company, 1/24th Regiment of Foot under Lieutenant Gonville Bromhead.

Unlike the sharp and sneering Michael Caine of the film, 'Gonny' was popular with the men but seen as benignly useless by his peers. Partially deaf and regarded as being lazy, his weaknesses in the field were carried by the regiment who made sure that he was always left in positions where he wouldn't be putting lives at risk. With Rorke's Drift safely behind the bulk of No.3 Column and B Company commander Captain Alfred Godwin Austen having been accidentally shot by one of his own men, defending the supply depot was the safest role available.

Bromhead's rock was Colour Sergeant Frank Bourne, who on the screen is depicted as the archetypal statuesque staff sergeant. In actuality, Bourne was 5' 5" tall, 23-years old and softly spoken, but he could read and write, and had such an affinity for army life that he scaled the ranks until he was giving orders to men his own age or older. The youngest NCO in the British Army, he was nicknamed 'The Kid'.

Also on hand were 100 poorly trained black auxiliaries of 2/3rd Natal Native Contingent under Captain William Stephenson, a colonial officer who spoke the local languages. He was supported by three black corporals but no white NCOs or

lieutenants, and the low combat effectiveness of his company - even by NNC standards - was probably why it was left at Rorke's Drift.

MAN THE BARRICADES

By noon on January 22, Chard had made it back to Rorke's Drift. He explained the situation at Isandlwana to Spalding and

ABOVE · Taken at his brother Cetshwayo kaMpande's coronation in 1873, the intemperate Dabulamanzi kaMpande stands at the centre of this photograph. He would go on to command the Zulu at the Battle of Rorke's Drift.
WELLCOME COLLECTION CC BY 4.0

impressed on him the vulnerability of their position. On the way in he had passed through Stephenson's men standing guard at the drift and opined that they would be quickly overwhelmed if the Zulu advanced on the mission. With approximately 200 defenders in all - and only half of them armed with Martini-Henry rifles - Rainforth's reinforcements were sorely needed.

Why he opted to leave rather than send a messenger hasn't been adequately explained, but Spalding decided to head ten miles up the road to Helpmekaar to hurry the reinforcements along. Just before he left, he paused and asked Chard who was the senior out of the two lieutenants, himself or Bromhead? (Stephenson was a colonial, and although he had equivalent rank, as

BELOW · B Company, 2nd Battalion, 24th Regiment of Foot - the gallant defenders of Rorke's Drift.

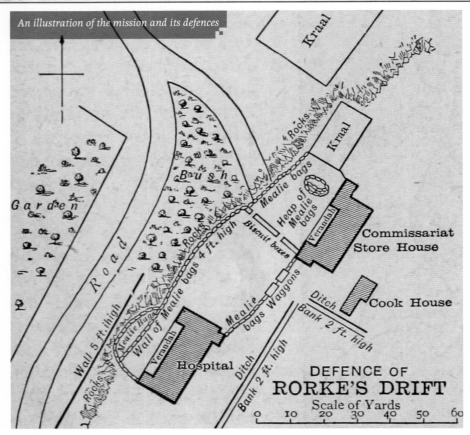

An illustration of the mission and its defences

DEFENCE OF RORKE'S DRIFT

Scale of Yards

a medic Reynolds couldn't command combat troops).

Chard confessed that he didn't know, so Spalding returned to his tent and dug out his copy of the *Army List* which revealed that Chard had been commissioned a lieutenant in 1868 and Bromhead in 1871. Under the old system, Bromhead purchased his commission of ensign in 1867, a junior rank that was phased out in 1871 resulting in an automatic promotion to lieutenant which wasn't exactly a glowing endorsement of Bromhead's abilities.

"You will be in charge, although of course nothing shall happen, and I shall be back again this evening early," said Spalding before he rode off. It was 2pm and those two promises would haunt them both in the hours that followed. For now, though, it was business as usual at Rorke's Drift and Chard went back to his tent by the pontoons for a spot of lunch.

At around 3.15pm, Witt, Reynolds and Smith - the missionary, the surgeon and the chaplain - were keeping watch from Oscarberg when they heard distant rifle fire and spotted Zulus crossing the Buffalo River into Natal. Thinking they were Natal Native Contingent at first, they did nothing until the sight of a settler farm being set alight shook them from their complacency. They rushed back to warn the camp with Smith bellowing, "Here they come! Thick as grass and black as Hell."

Part of the right horn of the Zulu attack had overshot Isandlwana in a broad sweep to discover the battle already won. Their blood was up, they had been cheated out of a role in the victory and their blades demanded to be fed. Three amaButho - two of which were made up of warriors in their 40s - under the command of Cetshwayo's half-brother, the aggressive and ambitious Dabulamanzi kaMpande, were heading for kwaJimu.

They had ignored the king's orders not to cross into Natal. Linking arms so not to be swept away by the fierce current, they had pushed across the Buffalo River south of Rorke's Drift in a human chain and were now sweeping north towards the mission. There was no great strategy at work. Dabulamanzi was simply marauding through the frontier with as many as 4,000 Zulu warriors in tow, looting farms and murdering survivors from Isandlwana.

The news had reached Chard and Bromhead already. Two riders had appeared from the direction of Isandlwana and raced towards Chard's crossing: one was a Natal Carbineer and the other introduced himself as Lieutenant Adendorff, 1/3rd Natal Native Contingent. Isandlwana had fallen, only a handful had managed to escape, and behind them a Zulu war party was bearing down on Rorke's Drift.

Back at the camp, Bromhead received message from Captain Edward Essex, one of the only staff officers to survive Isandlwana, with orders. They were to strengthen the defences and hold the mission at all costs. Bromhead dispatched a rider to the garrison

ABOVE · *John Chard pictured later in his career in the uniform of a major of the Royal Engineers. He's wearing his Victoria Cross.*

A photograph of Rorke's Drift taken after the battle showing the view from the northeast with the store and the stone kraal visible.

at Helpmekaar while Dalton, who had been trained in constructing field works, ordered the collapsing of the tents to offer a clear field of fire, the linking the two buildings with a perimeter of biscuit boxes and mealie bags, and the bashing firing holes into the walls of the hospital with pickaxes.

By the time Chard returned to exchange intelligence with Bromhead, the camp was already a whirlwind of activity. The officers were summoned to conference and Chard's prognosis was gloomy. He wanted the two wagons loaded and the garrison to vacate, but Dalton proved the voice of reason: if they left on foot, they would be overtaken by the Zulu and slaughtered on open ground. In contrast to the film which presents Chard as heroic from the outset, it was the semi-retired acting assistant commissary who strengthened the lieutenant's resolve to stand and fight. The wagons were emptied and added to the southern barricade.

While they returned to work, more ragged irregulars limped through the drift from Isandlwana "and tried to impress on us the madness of an attempt to defend the place," Chard recalled. "Who they were I do not know, but it is scarcely necessary for me to say there were no officers of HM army among them."

Though *Zulu* shows Adendorff staying to defend the mission, there's only one account that places him in the battle. In all likelihood, both Adendorff and the other trooper joined the ranks of retreating colonial volunteers.

THE LAST BETRAYAL

The flow of stragglers was punctuated by the stirring sight of an 80-man column of the elite Natal Native Horse led by Lieutenant Alfred Henderson who placed his troop at Chard's disposal. They had broken through the Zulu cordon and while other survivors had been forced towards Fugitives' Drift, they had charged straight down the road to Rorke's Drift.

The total number of defenders was now closer to 300. And Henderson's light horse was sent out as scouts around the drift and south face of Oscarberg with orders to delay the Zulu advance for a long as possible.

The pontoon briefly caused Chard some concern - it was after all his primary purpose. He decided to stake the pontoons in the centre of the Buffalo River and the two men responsible for manning the crossing - a civilian ferryman called Mr Daniells and Sergeant Frederick Milne, 2/3rd Regiment of Foot (The Buffs) - offered to stay and fight off any Zulu who tried to interfere. It was a near-suicidal commitment to duty even by the standards of the Victorian army and Chard dismissed it.

Linking up the hospital to the store left the defenders overstretched, but some of the patients could not be moved from their straw-lined cots. With the doors opening outwards from the hastily erected compound, Bromhead picked six men to defend the three exposed rooms - locking themselves in with ample ammunition to defend the patients. Those patients mobile enough to wield a rifle were to join the fight.

At 4.30pm B Company, those of the Natal Native Contingent with rifles, and a handful of the hospital's walking wounded were manning the perimeter with bayonets fixed. The NNC armed with assegai and cowhide shields sheltered in the stone cattle kraal. In front of the store a pyramid of unused mealie sacks towered over the defenders and Dalton had ordered a dozen boxes of ammunition opened so that the men could stuff their pouches with rounds.

Gunfire was heard around the south face of Oscarberg and at 4.30pm the Natal Native Horse raced past in full retreat, one of them shouting out in his native language that they were doomed, and the Zulu would be upon them. The mission's black auxiliaries panicked and bolted in their wake, and to the disgust of the defenders Stephenson joined them. As an irregular, he was unable to face court martial but his career as a colonial officer was over.

Colour Sergeant Bourne said later that "the desertion of these detachments of 200 men appeared at first sight to be a great loss, with only a hundred of us left, but the feeling afterwards was that we could not have trusted them, and also our defences were too small to accommodate them anyhow."

The reaction at the barricades was less temperate. One man shouted out "Come back here!" and shot a fleeing auxiliary in the back. Scattered gunfire was then heard as the NNC skirted the edge of the approaching Zulu.

Including the wounded and non-combatants, there were now 139 men left to hold Rorke's Drift against the oncoming foe.

BEATING THEM BACK

The first wave of Zulu - 600 men from the inDluyengwe regiment - crashed around Oscarberg and flung themselves at the southern wall of the field hospital and store. The defenders opened fire wildly at 500 yards but with the narrowest face of the mission towards the enemy, the Zulu made it to within 60 yards of the walls before they were torn to shreds by the firing line. 》》

Zulu warriors fling themselves at the barricade. At points, the piles of dead were so deep that the Zulu could scramble up them to clear the mealie bags.

A larger chunk of the attackers veered left around the hospital to the northwestern corner of the stockade where they pressed right up to the barricade itself through sheer concentrated force of numbers. Bromhead, wielding his revolver, and Dalton with a rifle led the fierce hand-to-hand. Among his many skills, Dalton was a superb marksman and shot down a Zulu poised to run through a member of the Army Hospital Corps whose rifle had been knocked aside. The pressure was such that the defenders were forced back towards the front of the hospital, their bayonets held steadily forward.

Private Henry Hitch who had been keeping watch on the hospital roof and slid down to join the scrap, recalled:

"Had the Zulus taken to the bayonet as freely as they took to the bullets, we could not have stood more than 15 minutes. They pushed right up to us and not only got up to the laager but got in with us. But they seemed to have a great deal of dread of the bayonet, which stood us from beginning to end."

sheltering the garden, and another group of Zulus in the stone kraal to the northeast also peppered the barricades with gunfire.

The men on the mountain had an almost unrestricted line of fire over the camp, and had they been even half the shots that B Company were, the mission would have soon fallen. So heavily outnumbered were the defenders that a single massed charge on all sides would have easily overwhelmed them but lurking behind a tree to avoid giving British snipers a target had resulted in Dabulamanzi having poor visibility over the battlefield.

Nonetheless, the hospital was correctly identified as the weakest point in the defence - not only because of its fewer firing positions, but because of the difficulty in bringing more defenders to bear, although the Zulus would likely not have known about the lack of internal doors.

As the light began to fade, the Zulus kept up their assault on the hospital and the northwest wall. Corporal Christian Schiess, a Swiss-born NCO in the Natal Native Contingent and not an officer of the

Natal Mounted Police as the film claims, had limped from the hospital to join the defenders on the barricade. A powerfully built veteran of the Franco-Prussian War (1870-1871), he proved himself a demon with the bayonet.

Chaplain Smith made the rounds too. He was unable to bear arms, but he worked his way around the line distributing ammunition and asking the men not to swear so much, which earned him both respect, mirth and the nickname 'Ammunition Smith.'

Chard recalled: "Each time, as the attack was repulsed by us, the Zulus close to us seemed to vanish into the bush, those some little distance off keeping up a fire all the time. Then, as if moved by a single impulse, they rose up in the bush as thick as possible, rushing madly up to the wall. Some of them being already close to it, seizing where they could, the muzzles of our men's rifles, or their bayonets, and attempting to use their assegais and to get over the wall. A rapid rattle of fire from our rifles, stabs with the bayonets, and in a few moments the Zulus were driven back, disappearing in the bush as before, and keeping up their fire."

THE HOSPITAL AFLAME

At 6pm, Dabulamanzi ordered the last major push of the day: a simultaneous offensive on both the south and north walls. It was the sort of coordinated action that the defenders had been dreading, and Chard ordered the men back behind an inner wall of biscuit boxes between the store and the hospital that reduced the perimeter by two thirds. It was either that or risk the mission being

ABOVE · *Some of the survivors of B Company not repatriated through injury or illness. On the bottom row are Lieutenant Chard (far right, with the dog) and Lieutenant Bromhead (far left), and Private Hook is at the back middle with a rifle and beard.*

RIGHT · *The defenders of Rorke's Drift sheltering behind mealie bags.*

A warrior tossed his weapons aside and grabbed Hitch's rifle by the barrel, trying to pull it from the soldier's grasp. Clinging on to the butt for dear life, Hitch pushed a round into the breech and shot the Zulu at point blank range.

Under the fierce defence and covering fire from the hospital, the first wave melted away and disappeared behind the wall of the garden to the northwest of the mission. By now hundreds of Zulu were scattered on the southern face of Oscarberg, firing down on Rorke's Drift from behind rocks and caves with the rifles they had taken from Isandlwana. The men

Understandably much focus is given to the unprecedented 11 Victoria Crosses awarded at Rorke's Drift, and indeed you can read more about them on page 102, so we would like to pay tribute to the men behind the four Distinguished Conduct Medals, as well as the forgotten fifth man whose award was forfeited.

The DCM was introduced by Royal Warrant on December 4, 1854 during the Crimean War (1853-1856) to recognise the 'distinguished, gallant and good conduct in the field' of warrant officers, NCOs and enlisted men. It was the second highest gallantry award after the VC and the equivalent of the Distinguished Service Order, which was only available to commissioned officers. Prior to the DCM, there was no award for single acts of heroism and men awarded the DCM were entitled to an annuity payment following their discharge.

Colour Sergeant Frank Bourne was awarded the DCM and a £10 annuity for 'outstanding coolness and courage' during the battle. It was just the start of a long career that saw 'The Kid' become quartermaster-sergeant and then adjutant of the School of Musketry in Dublin, a post he returned to during the First World War. At the end of the war, he was given the honorary rank of lieutenant-colonel and an OBE. A fitting bookend to his service, in the wake of Rorke's Drift he was offered a commission but was unable to afford it. Bourne passed away May 8, 1945 aged 91 at his home in Beckenham. His campaign medals can be seen at the Regimental Museum of The Royal Welsh, Brecon.

Second-Corporal Francis Attwood, Army Service Corps was awarded the DCM and a promotion to sergeant for his role in the defence. The only member of ASC at the mission, Attwood prevented the store going

Above · Following the death of Queen Victoria, the coat of arms was replaced by the profile of the reigning monarch until 1993 when the award was phased out.

Left · Frank Bourne sometime before 1900, wearing the uniform of a captain and carrying the cocked hat of a specialist. This is most likely from his time as adjutant.

the same way as the hospital and from his vantage point at the only window shot down a Zulu trying to set the thatch alight. Attwood died February 20, 1884 aged 38 following an epileptic fit. His medals are held by the Royal Logistic Corps Museum, Surrey.

Gunner John Cantwell, No.5 Royal Artillery was most likely left at Rorke's Drift as a storeman for the battery's supplies. His exact role in the defence is unknown, but he went on to serve in Malta and India before being discharged in 1887 as medically unfit for service. In 1892 he returned to Natal and served as a prison officer in Durban and then prison warden in Pietermaritzburg. He died August 14, 1900 from complications of an enlarged spleen aged 53.

One of the hospital patients recovering from malaria, Private John William Roy, 1/24th Regiment of Foot was awarded the DCM and a promotion to corporal for his part in defending the hospital and helping the wounded escape.

His early history was a tragic one, blighted by alcohol, desertion and syphilis, and his death was just as sad. Roy emigrated to Australia in 1883 and by 1887 he was described as 'almost blind, and helpless' and living in a 'benevolent institution.' He died May 30, 1890 aged 35 and was buried in an unmarked grave.

An equally tragic story surrounds Private Michael McMahon, Army Hospital Corps. One of the three orderlies assisting Surgeon Reynolds, McMahon dashed out into the line of fire to help one of the patients out of the hospital window during the fire. McMahon's early army record is a sorry tale of drunkenness and imprisonment and his DCM was cancelled in January 1880 following desertion and theft (presumably he absconded with army property) on November 14, 1879. The details of his later life are unknown, but even the gallantry of rogues deserves to be remembered.

entirely overrun, but Chard's decision left six soldiers and 24 wounded stranded in the besieged hospital building.

Now surrounding the hospital on three sides, the Zulu flung flaming assegai after flaming assegai onto the sodden thatch until it caught light. The only external door which hadn't been barricaded ahead of the battle opened onto the veranda which was now firmly in Zulu hands.

In the southeast corner room was a single NNC warrior with broken legs and Privates Henry Hook and Robert Cole, who fired through their loopholes into the attacking Zulu. Unlike the unscrupulous rogue of

Zulu - created presumably for the sake of having a redemptive character arc - the real Hook was an upstanding soldier, lay preacher and teetotaller. He wasn't in the hospital as a malingerer, but as the cook. Cole bolted early on, but Hook held firm.

"The helpless patient was crying and groaning near me," said Hook. "The Zulus were swarming around us, and there was an extraordinary rattle as the bullets struck the biscuit boxes, and queer thumps as they plumped into the bags of mealie."

The outer door was covered by a mattress and a stack of mealie sacks, and as smoke began to fill the room Hook broke through

the inner door and left the immobile African levy to his death. He was confronted by nine more patients and unwilling to leave them to their fate, he sealed up the door he had come through just as the Zulu burst into the room behind him and slaughtered the wounded soldier in his cot.

In another room, Privates John and Joseph Williams had been defending four patients. No relation, B Company had several men named Jones and Williams, but its 'Welsh' character has been severely overstated. Although the 24th Regiment had moved to Brecon in 1873, many of the men had been recruited from the industrial

Midlands. There would be no throaty renditions of 'Men of Harlech'.

Theirs was one of the rooms with no internal door and when their ammunition ran out, Joseph Jones and two of the patients had been dragged from the room by the Zulu while the others hacked at the internal wall of crude mud and brick with their bayonets. From there, Jones dug his way into Hook's new location.

Hook and Williams now had 11 patients, a shoddily reinforced door through which the Zulu could break in and only one possible route of escape: making another

William Jones were protecting six patients. While the two Joneses covered the door with their bayonets, Hook and Williams lowered the patients six feet from a high northeast-facing window to the ground where they could make a dash across the 40-yard killing field for the inner wall of biscuit boxes. With the defenders offering covering fire, most of them made it.

One man had been missed - Private Waters had hidden in a cupboard and Hook had moved right past him - and another couldn't be moved. Sergeant Maxwell had been dressed but in his feverish delirium

nervous of fighting at night. From a purely practical standpoint, command and control were impossible when the iNduna couldn't see what his warriors were doing, but there were supernatural threats too. In the darkness malign forces called umnyama cast their baleful presence on the deeds of men.

The concentrated offensives of the afternoon became a series of probing attacks. The hospital burned for hours, its glow aiding the British in picking their targets. Trooper Harry Lugg, one of the walking wounded from the Natal Mounted Police recalled: "The thatch roof burst out

Less well known than Neuville's painting, The Defense of Rorke's Drift by Elizabeth Thompson, Lady Butler similarly shows the battle's significant individuals. In the middle Lieutenant Bromhead holds his sword and follows Lieutenant Chard's direction.

hole in another wall. While Hook covered the door with his bayonet, Williams took a pickaxe to the far wall. By now the internal door was open and one at a time, the Zulu were trying to force their way in. An assegai glanced off the regimental crest on Hook's sun helmet and a warrior leapt forward to grab the barrel of his Martini-Henry. Hook wrenched it from his grasp and shot the Zulu dead.

"All this time Williams was getting the sick through the hole into the next one," recalled Hook. "All except one, a soldier of the 24th named Private John Conley, who could not move because of a broken leg. Watching my chance, I dashed for the doorway and, grabbing Conley, I pulled him after me through the hole. His leg got broken again, but there was no help for it. As soon as we left the room the Zulus burst in with furious cries of disappointment and rage."

Hook and Williams pushed through into the next room and then the room beyond, in which Private Robert and Private

he was thrashing about. They were forced to leave him, and he was stabbed to death where he lay. The Joneses had fought valiantly to protect their charges. Robert had been stabbed three times and was growing weak with blood loss, only the spread of fire saved him - throwing its orange curtain between the Zulu and the soldiers so that William could help Robert through the window.

On the other side of the field hospital, another patient - Gunner Arthur Howard - had died when part of the burning roof collapsed in on him. Private Robert Adams, 2/24th had been defending the same room, but he managed to slip out into the night and hide among the dead. Waters too was able to disappear in the darkness. Chased from his cupboard by the smoke, he caked his face in soot and hid in the abandoned cookhouse to wait out the battle.

TOOTH AND NAIL

Though buoyed by the sight of the burning field hospital, the Zulu were traditionally

into flames and made it as light as day, and before they had time to retreat we were pouring bullets into them like hail. We could see them falling in scores. Then you could hear suppressed British cheers."

On the far side of the mission from the hospital, the Zulu managed to drive the defenders from the small stone kraal abutting the northeastern barricade.

Acting Assistant Commissary Dalton was leading the defence of a seven-yard gap in the biscuit box wall and by Chard's reckoning "had been using his rifle to deadly effect, and by his quickness and coolness had been the means of saving many men's lives." Finally shot in the shoulder, Dalton handed his rifle to Chard with such calmness that "I had no idea until afterwards how severely he was wounded."

Corporal Schiess, distinguished himself too. Walking wounded already, the Swiss man vaulted the wall to bayonet a Zulu who had shot his helmet off, two more warriors ran at him and he shot one and stabbed the other. Later hit by a bullet that incredibly bounced off the back of his head and lodged in his shoulder, he continued to fight.

Private Hitch was shot too - a slug from a muzzle-loaded musket shattered his shoulder bone. Finding that his right arm would no longer move he tucked it into his belt and traded his rifle for Lieutenant Bromhead's revolver so that he could continue to fight, saying, "I did as much execution [then] as I had done before." Four hours later, Hitch passed out from blood loss and was taken to Reynolds.

Even within this reduced fortification and greater concentration of fire, the Zulu stood poised to overrun Rorke's Drift and Assistant Commissary Dunne set out arranging the stack of unused mealie bags into a final circular redoubt for the defenders - the result stood 20 feet high and 12 feet wide.

The men fought on, deafened by the din of discharging rifles, their throats hoarse and dry from the smoke and the shouting. Shoulders and biceps were bruised from the kick of the rifle a hundred times over, and many soldiers had swapped to their off hands to share the punishment with their opposite shoulders. Fingers were burnt from the overheated barrels - and one or two could be seen gently glowing in the dark - and some men had powder burns on their faces.

By now the Zulu appetite for battle was fading. They were getting spooked by reports that a British relief column was closing in on Rorke's Drift - indeed Brevet Major Spalding was on his way back with two companies from Helpmekaar, gathering up refugees from Isandlwana en route and adding them to the force.

As it happened, Spalding was to abandon Rorke's Drift twice. When they sighted the burning field hospital in the distance, the major decided that the mission had already fallen and turned his relief column back to Helpmekaar.

By 4.30am the Zulu guns had fallen silent.

COUNTING THE COST

As dawn broke over the smouldering mission, the defenders were stunned to see the Zulu army returning around the foot of Oscarberg, from where they had originally come.

Seventeen defenders were dead, many more wounded - some seriously, but beyond the stockade lay heaps of Zulu dead. That they had spent 20,000 rounds of ammunition accounted for this staggering loss of life. Cautiously sending men out to gather the weapons they counted 351 Zulu dead.

Hundreds more Zulu would die within days, lacking the medical knowledge to care for bullet wounds. The death toll would be difficult to account. The Zulu practice of

Mounted Infantry from Chelmsford's column cheer as they arrive at Rorke's Drift on the morning of January 23. This illustration is a copy of a rough sketch by an eyewitness.

ABOVE · *Lieutenant John Chard's .45 Webley RIC revolver used at Rorke's Drift, currently on display at the Royal Engineers Museum in Gillingham, Kent.* JLEDDEN CC BY-SA 4.0

retiring to the warrior's home kraal for ritual purification following a battle obscured the casualties to the extent that it was possible for Dabulamanzi to conceal the scale of the defeat from the king for weeks, reporting his 'great victory' in taking the hospital.

An estimated 500 other Zulu casualties would be butchered where they lay shivering among the dead. After the last ten hours - and the massacre at Isandlwana - mercy had been exhausted.

At 8am a cheer went up as Chelmsford's column was spotted coming from the direction of Isandlwana. The men hugged each other in relief and a signal flag was waved from the roof of the storehouse.

Within minutes Mounted Infantry rode past waving their helmets and cheering and following them was Chelmsford.

Chard presented his report to the general, and then Chelmsford insisted on meeting some of the heroes of the night. He went on to make 11 recommendations for the Victoria Cross - the largest number ever awarded in a single action by one regiment - along with four Distinguished Conduct Medals.

Chelmsford's gloomy mood at not finding Rorke's Drift thronged with survivors from Isandlwana had been lifted when he realised the scale of the victory. A heroic stand against all odds might be just the thing to rescue his reputation after the massacre of the previous day.

One man captured the mood from the bottom of the pile. Private Robert Head found a stub of pencil and a scrap of charred paper and wrote to his brother in Cape Town:

"I dare say the old fool in command will make great fuss of the two officers commanding our company in keeping the Zulu buck back with the private soldier, but what will [the private soldier] get? Nothing, only he may get the praise of the public."

Chelmsford's cynicism and careerism does nothing to diminish the heroism and success of the Rorke's Drift's defenders, especially in contrast to Isandlwana. Early that same day poor leadership, misreading of the signs, and lack of fortifications resulted in a very different outcome for what is a strikingly similar balance of odds.

With everyone busy, Chard dug out a bottle of beer he had hidden away and shared it with Bromhead. ◖◖◖▬

STEADY THE BUFFS

The Siege of Eshowe, January 22-April 3, 1879

COLONEL PEARSON.

ABOVE LEFT · *Colonel Charles Knight Pearson*

ABOVE · *A Naval Brigade gun crew practice with the Gatling gun at Fort Pearson on the Natal bank of the Tugela River.*

Colonel Charles Knight Pearson and No.1 Column had been in the process of fortifying the mission station of Eshowe for six days when news arrived. On January 28, at approximately noon, a rider galloped up the road from Fort Tenedos with a message from Lord Chelmsford: No.3 Column was retiring, and Pearson was on his own.

Chelmsford's orders, such as they were, read: "Consider all my instructions as cancelled, and act in whatever manner you think most desirable in the interests of the column under your command. Should you consider the garrison of Eshowe as too far advanced to be fed safely, you can withdraw it [...] You must be prepared to have the whole Zulu force down upon you."

It was only on February 7 that the full scale of the slaughter at Isandlwana became clear, and Pearson summoned a council of senior officers to vote on whether to stay or go.

Captain Warren Wynne, Royal Engineers came out most strongly for holding tight. He argued that retreat would leave them vulnerable to attack, whereas holding a strongly fortified position would tie up a significantly larger force of Zulu and leave them with a beachhead once the invasion resumed. Their decision was aided by the arrival of fresh supplies and the senior officers agreed.

No.1 was the largest of the three main columns with a professional core of two British infantry battalions - 2/3rd Regiment of Foot (The Buffs) and 99th Duke of Edinburgh's (Lanarkshire) Regiment of Foot - and a Naval Brigade of 290 sailors with small arms, 24-pounder Hales rocket tubes and a Gatling gun. A small detachment of Royal Artillery also provided fire support with two 7-pounder mountain guns and a smaller 9-pounder Hales rocket trough.

Also attached were 312 colonial cavalry raised in Natal - No.2 Squadron Mounted Infantry, Natal Hussars, Durban Mounted Rifles, Alexandra Mounted Rifles, Stanger Mounted Rifles, and Victoria Mounted Rifles - and 2nd Regiment Natal Native Contingent. In the rear were engineers and pioneers, plus a train of 384 wagons, 24 carts, and 3,128 oxen. The total manpower was 4,750.

Despite the capabilities of his force, Pearson was the least experienced column commander - he had last seen action in the Crimean War (1853-1856) and had floated around several staff posts, retiring just prior to the outbreak of the Anglo-Zulu War which drew him back to the colours.

THE BATTLE OF NEYEZANE

After crossing Lower Drift into Zululand on January 12, Pearson's orders were to advance 30 miles north to Eshowe and use

it as a forward post for the big push towards Ulundi, the royal kraal of King Cetshwayo kaMpande. A fort was immediately constructed on the Zulu bank of the Tugela River to protect the drift - Fort Tenedos - and in a moment of self-indulgence, the fort on the Natal bank was renamed Fort Pearson.

Unlike Chelmsford, Pearson had immediately fortified his beachhead, but like the general, his progress slumped to a crawl in the rain-sodden earth and his intelligence was poor. Scouts warned him that a single iButho had been sent to oppose him, but as the Zulu marched south they gathered up reinforcements from the main Zulu army as well as local kraals to assemble a force of over 6,000 warriors.

It was only sheer dumb luck that prevented a disaster to echo the one that was about to unfold in the northwest. As Pearson's advance party camped on the night of January 21, the Zulu got skittish. The local chief thought the sound of British sentries calling to each other was a sign that a trap was being set, and he led his army further north to confront them two miles further up the road where the tall reeds of the Neyezane valley and deserted kraal crowning Wombane Hill would give them the advantage.

Good fortune spared Pearson from humiliation a second time. While the Zulu were preparing their ambush, a forward patrol of NNC spotted the left horn of the enemy clearing the ridge of Wombane Hill and filtering into the bush to the right of the road.

Captain Fitzroy Hart, 1/2nd NNC recalled: "I instantly gave the order 'Retire'. At the same moment, the Zulus poured down the hill by hundreds at the top of their speed, with a tremendous shout, while others above kept up the fire over the heads of those descending the hill."

Immediately, the British moved up to engage in front of No.1 Column. Though the Zulu held the high ground ahead of them where the road wound through the hills, their premature charge left them with a far greater distance to close. The artillery took up positions on a small knoll facing the bulk of the Zulu force, along with two companies of Buffs.

The wagons continued to pull up and park to form a laager, while the men on the knoll provided covering fire. As »»

ABOVE · *The Gatling gun enters combat at the Battle of Neyezane, shattering the left horn of the Zulu advance.*

ABOVE RIGHT · *Skirmish lines of Zulu advance through the undergrowth to harry the defenders of Fort Eshowe.*

RIGHT · *Lieutenant Charles Hayes, Royal Engineers is shown communicating with Eshowe via heliograph from Fort Tenedos. In actuality, Hayes used a heliostat where the flashing Morse code is created by obscuring the sun and not turning the mirror.*

the Zulu left horn in the surrounding scrub took pot-shots at the column, two companies of Buffs moving up with the wagons were ordered to drive them into the open where the men on the knoll could pick them off. They were assisted by the cavalry and half a company of 99th.

Finally, the Gatling gun arrived from the rear and set up on the knoll to join the rockets where it was fired in anger by British forces for the first time. The left horn beaten back, the Zulu right horn was forced into a desperate flanking manoeuvre. A naval officer described the closing stage of the engagement:

"The Zulus advancing on our left, the bluejackets [navy] were ordered there, and being very exposed moving up the road, four of our men were wounded. Driving the enemy along the road and being supported by two companies of the Buffs under Colonel [Henry] Parnell, we charged up the hill when the Zulus took flight."

By 9.30am the battle was over. More than 300 warriors were dead and many more wounded. The British had suffered only ten dead and 17 wounded, two mortally so. After camping on a small ridge, at 10am on January 23 they reached Eshowe and Chelmsford's grim tidings followed in their wake.

DIGGING IN

The oldest European settlement in Zululand, Eshowe, had - like Rorke's Drift - been acquired as a Norwegian mission station. It consisted of a church, a school and a house, and was surrounded on three sides by low hills that rose over the station and on the fourth side by a bush-covered ravine. The location had been chosen because of its access to running water and its vulnerability to the encircling high ground wasn't a factor to the men of God who settled it in 1861.

"How calm, how peaceful, it all looked when we marched in that bright morning," wrote an anonymous officer, describing his experiences in *Blackwood's Magazine* (July-December 1879). "Now soon to be converted into as hideous a spot as there was in Zululand!"

The question of provisions obliged Pearson to send 2nd Natal Native Contingent and the colonial cavalry back to Fort Tenedos. Armed with spears and only one rifle between 10 men, the 2,000 black auxiliaries would be of limited use holding the firing line, and the column didn't have enough grain to feed the horses of the 312 irregulars. Reducing the number of combatants at Eshowe to around 1,300 (plus 400 native pioneers) also increased the available ammunition to 320 rounds per man.

No.2 Natal Native Pioneers and No.2 Royal Engineers went to work. Trenches were dug, and sloping revetments of earth and timber ramparts were built over six feet high, with firing steps and bastions. These were surrounded by a six-foot ditch lined with sharpened stakes and the men on the walls habitually tossed bottles over so that the shards of broken glass would do their bit to deter barefooted attackers. A lattice of wire was also staked into the ground on the approach, designed to slow a charge.

Within the 150 yards by 50-yard compound, the wagons were laagered around the buildings as a redoubt - a second wall from which to fight if the first were overrun. Tents were taken down and the men slept under the wagons. A field hospital was set up in the church, firing holes were knocked into the walls, and the bell tower became a watchtower.

THE HARD MONTHS

The great assault on Fort Eshowe never came. If the defenders had learnt from Isandlwana, then perhaps the attackers had learnt from Rorke's Drift.

The Zulu were content to wait it out. Either the British would be forced to leave and fight on open ground, or they would starve to death. Over the two months of the siege, the Zulu watched and waited from the hills. They probed the defences, creeping through the ravine to assault the walls. By day, British patrols prowled the surrounding countryside fighting occasional skirmishes and the Zulu made constant attempts to steal the oxen while they grazed under the eyes of a company of infantry. By night, the pickets returned, and the livestock were penned in the moat.

It was a war of discomfort, rather than attrition. By night the Zulu would chop down the trees that the pickets had sheltered under the previous day and move range markers - at least until Wynne discouraged them by rigging the wooden stakes with dynamite.

So twitchy grew the defenders that the Natal Native Pioneers had to wear a square of blue cloth, so they could be identified as friendly, and they were forbidden from roaming beyond the walls during the day. When the overwhelming Zulu attack failed to materialise, the fort was continually developed until it included a wooden drawbridge over the trench and firing platforms to give the 7-pounders and the Gatling gun the greatest possible field of fire.

As the Zulu tightened their grip around the countryside, messengers stopped getting through and Wynne considered several solutions to reach out to Fort Tenedos, 20 miles away. First, he improvised a paper balloon to carry messages, but that was too dependent on the wind. Then he experimented with a large sheet of tarpaulin on a wooden frame that when viewed through binoculars could be used to signal in Morse. This too was frustrated by the wind which collapsed the frame like an umbrella in a storm.

Finally, Wynne rigged up a heliograph from a piece of mirror and lead piping, and the garrisons of Fort Tenedos and Fort Pearson did the same (until Chelmsford sent signallers up with a heliostat). Provided the sun was shining, the heliograph could flash Morse back and forth. At first, it was used for military business only, but as the siege dragged on the men were charged five shillings to send personal messages before this risked cluttering up the vital lines of communication.

FAR LEFT · *A Zulu scout creeps through the bush to maintain the pressure on the defenders of Fort Eshowe.*

LEFT · *One of the many unmarked British graves at Fort Pearson, where many of the sick of Eshowe passed away following the lifting of the siege.* WITSTINKHOUT CC BY-SA 3.0

BOTTOM · *The ramparts of Fort Eshowe.*

So long as the British held firm within the stockade, dysentery and enteric fever were deadlier foes than the Zulu, accounting for at least 20 of the 31 deaths. Sleeping on the ground, muddy after the rains, and covered in waste from the column's animals, Fort Eshowe was cramped, claustrophobic and unsanitary. The field hospital began to fill up so fast that Staff Surgeon Henry Frederick Norbury, Royal Navy exhausted his medicines and raided the veterinary stores instead. When that was emptied he began to experiment with infusions of tree bark.

Pearson cut rations in half to keep the men going until April, and by April they were subsisting on stringy oxen and smoking used tea leaves, but the end was in sight. From their vantage point, they could see miles, from the shimmering Indian Ocean in the east to the glimmering heliostat of Fort Tenedos in the south, and they watched the cluster of campfires that marked Lord Chelmsford's relief column grow steadily closer.

In the end, the siege would end with a whimper, the bang occurring elsewhere as a force of 11,000 Zulu were defeated at nearby Gingindlovu on April 2, 1879.

The most impressive fortification of the conflict was never put to the test. It could be argued that it was an effective deterrent, that no Zulu chief dared see the field littered with the bodies of his warriors. Equally, it could be argued that the Siege of Eshowe was a Zulu victory, as the largest British column in the field was locked uselessly away in a prison of its own devising for over three months.

Struck by fever in March, the ingenious and indefatigable Captain Warren Wynne passed away on April 9, 1879 aged 36. Colonel Pearson blamed his death in part on "unflinchingly remaining at his duty when almost incapable of performing it."

Wynne was promoted to major posthumously.

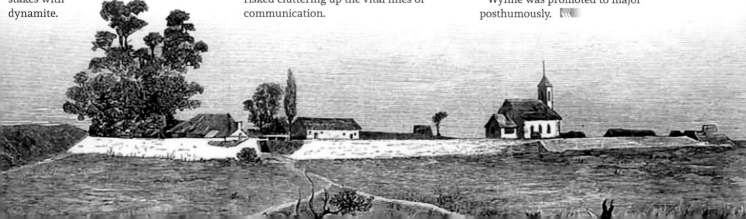

KILLERS IN THE MIST

The Battle of Intombe, March 12, 1879

The defenders of the laager put up more of a fight in this illustration than they would have been able to at the time, the Zulu springing on them out of the morning mist. Nonetheless, it captures the ferocity and desperation of the fighting.

The failures of No.1 and No.3 Column startled Colonel Rowland's small No.5 Column standing guard in Transvaal. Not only did they have Zulu to worry about over the eastern frontier, but the Boers were taking advantage of the distracted Brits and there were murmurings of insurrection in the grasslands of the Highveld.

Most vulnerable to the Zulu were the settlements in the Disputed Territory. Vital as they were to public opinion in the ornery Transvaal, they had to be defended at all costs, particularly the town of Lüneberg which was a matter of miles from the kraal of Chief Mbilini waMswati, an exiled Swazi prince with nominal loyalty to the Zulu king.

ABOVE · *Colour Sergeant Anthony Booth wearing his Victoria Cross. He had been promoted to colour sergeant in 1876 but reverted to sergeant in February 1879. After the action at Intombe, he was restored to his earlier rank.*

On February 18, Brevet Major Charles Tucker and four companies of 80th Regiment of Foot (Staffordshire Volunteers) arrived to garrison Lüneberg. The supply lines through the Disputed Territory were fraught, the roads unsteady, the River Intombe unpredictable in foul weather, and the nearby Zulu a constant threat.

Dumping the Wagons

As the rain poured down on March 5, feeding the Intombe and turning the ground to slush, a train of 18 wagons laden with 90,000 rounds of ammunition and other supplies became trapped on the wrong side of the river. The lead wagon was stuck part way through Myer's Drift and a number of wagons had piled up behind it, while others had run into difficulties of their own and were scattered miles back.

The escort of 80th had been ordered to make Lüneberg 'at any cost.' Fearful of the Zulu taking advantage as they skidded

around in the mud, the company commander abandoned the wagons to the encroaching darkness and the pummelling rain.

By morning the river had burst its banks and the drift could not be crossed by wagon, a party succeeded in freeing only the lead wagon on March 6. The plan was to recover all the ammunition wagons at least, but unloading the lead wagon, carrying the ammunition to the shore, and then pulling the empty wagon free used up all the light.

The following day, Tucker ordered Captain David Moriarty to take 100 men of H Company, retrieve the stricken wagon from the flooded drift, round up all the other wagons that were scattered further down the route, and laager them on the far banks of the Intombe until the water level dropped.

Moriarty had served for three years in southern Africa already and was, as far as Tucker was concerned, a perfectly capable commander for such a vital mission.

Cruel Awakening

On March 11 during a break in the torrential rain, Tucker rode out to the laager and was not impressed. Half the force was camped on

ABOVE · *A typical Boer ox wagon crossing a drift. Fully laden, the wagons were slow moving and required huge teams of oxen to haul them.*

the Lüneberg side of the bank, and the other half was camped around the laager on the opposite side.

Moriarty had assembled the wagons in a 'v' shape, with the open mouth to the river - but as the water slowly receded it exposed a growing gap. Furthermore, the wagons were spaced too far apart, which again left gaps that the Zulu could exploit. It was too close to evening for anything to be done and as he left Tucker was reassured at least that the ammunition wagons were in the centre of the laager with the oxen.

At 3.30am on the morning of March 12 mist clung to Intombe. The crack of a rifle woke the camp from its fitful slumber, but Moriarty could see nothing untoward and ordered the men to stand down and return to their tents or their blankets beneath the wagons. By 5am the mist had cleared to

reveal hundreds of Zulu advancing silently on the laager, and the sentries sounded the alarm, but it was too late, the Zulu fired a thunderous volley and then charged.

Tucker reported "[The Zulu] were around the wagons, and on top of them, and even inside with the cattle, almost instantly. So quickly did they come, there was really no defence on the part of our men; it was simply each man fighting for his life, and in a very few minutes all was over, our men being simply slaughtered."

Moriarty, revolver in hand, killed three warriors before a spear was plunged into his back. Staggering towards the laager, he was shot and sunk to his knees shouting, "I'm done! Fire away, boys! Death or glory!" Those lucky enough to gather their wits before death rushed in among them tumbled towards the river, where Lieutenant Henry Harwood, Sergeant Anthony Booth and the men on the Lüneberg bank gave cover. Sergeant Booth recalled: "We at once opened fire, and kept the fire up for about ten minutes or quarter of an hour, the [Zulus] were then in the river in great numbers coming towards us."

Harwood issued orders to retreat and then fled the field, taking the only horse available and leaving his men behind him. Booth, having command fall upon him through death and cowardice, drew up some of the men and formed a fighting rear guard, keeping the Zulu at bay with volley fire while the half-dressed, soaking wet survivors of the laager headed for a deserted farm two miles away.

This action saw Booth awarded the Victoria Cross. Thanks to his leadership, 40 of his comrades survived. Harwood meanwhile galloped into Lüneberg, woke Tucker and fainted on the spot. He was later court martialled and although acquitted, Harwood's career in the army was over having been scapegoated for panicking in a disaster not of his making.

"As we approached the Intombe Drift a fearful and horrible sight presented itself," recalled Tucker, "and the stillness of the spot was awful; there were our men lying all about the place, some naked and some only half clad. On the opposite side of the drift, I need not attempt to describe to you what I saw; all the bodies were full of assegai wounds and nearly all of them were disembowelled."

Over 60 men of the 80th Regiment of Foot had been slaughtered, along with 15 black ox drivers, and two white wagon conductors. The supplies had been either looted or destroyed. The Zulu dead numbered only 30.

THE DEVIL'S MOUNTAIN

The Battle of Hlobane, March 28, 1879

Though the men of No.4 Column may not have realised it, they were blessed to fight under two of the most capable senior officers in Africa. Brevet Colonel Evelyn Wood, VC, CB and Lieutenant Colonel Redvers Buller were part of the 'Wolseley Ring' that had gathered around the energetic army reformer Sir Garnet Wolseley during the 3rd Ashanti War (1873-1874).

The mountainous north of Zululand was home to chiefs who formally paid homage to King Cetshwayo kaMpande of the Zulu but were to varying degrees their own men.

These unpredictable local warlords would have to either be broken or won over to the British cause and the hope was that Wood would be able to turn a significant number of tribes against their monarch.

He would need them. No.4 Column was the smallest of the three invasion forces, with just over 2,000 men overall - 1,500 of them infantry of 90th Regiment of Foot (Perthshire Volunteers) and 13th (1st Somersetshire) (Prince Albert's Light Infantry) Regiment of Foot. In support, Wood could call on six 7-pounders and 100 men of 11/7th Battery, Royal Artillery.

Though there were significantly fewer irregulars than the other columns, most of the 200 cavalry were the Frontier Light Horse, commanded by Buller, and a Boer detachment under Piet Uys whose hatred of the Zulus outweighed their hatred of the British. Finally, the 300-strong Wood's Irregulars (50 of them mounted) came from tribes hostile to the Zulu and were under the command of Major William Knox-Leet.

ABOUT FACE

Having successfully accepted the submission of a local chief, Wood concentrated on

The wide plateau of Hlobane Mountain dwarfing the kraals in the foreground.

ABOVE · *Fighting for their lives, the Mounted Infantry stumble down the deadly Devil's Pass, the Zulu and their abaQulusi allies in full pursuit.*

LEFT · *Brevet Colonel Henry Evelyn Wood, VC, CB, in 1878, drawn just prior to the outbreak of the Anglo-Zulu War. Wood arrived in southern Africa in January 1878 for the final phase of the 9th Frontier War.*

trying to pacify the abaQulusi tribe, who risked menacing their left flank from their mountain redoubts of Zungwini and Hlobane 10 miles to the north.

When stealing their cattle and attempting to ransom them back to the abaQulusi chief - Sikhobobo - failed to yield the desired result, Buller led his Frontier Light Horse and some of Piet Uys's Boers to Zungwini on January 20, fighting ⫸

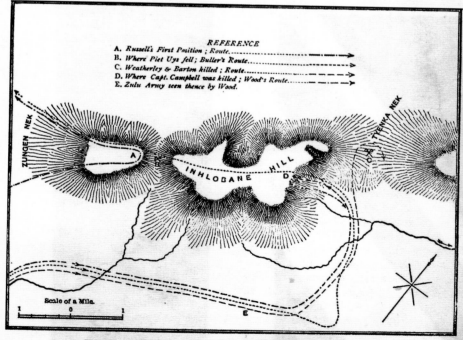

REFERENCE
A. *Russell's First Position ; Route.*
B. *Where Piet Uys fell ; Buller's Route.*
C. *Weatherley & Barton killed ; Route.*
D. *Where Capt. Campbell was killed ; Wood's Route.*
E. *Zulu Army seen thence by Wood.*

PLAN OF THE FIGHT ON THE INHLOBANE MOUNTAIN (MARCH 28, 1879).

their way up the narrow cattle track to the plateau. There the irregulars found a considerable abaQulusi force, and after losing around a dozen men in the offensive were forced to retreat.

As night fell on January 21, Wood took the 90th Regiment, two of the 7-pounders and the cavalry, and at first light the following day they crept up the slope to the kraal on Zungwini. Thanks to Buller and Uys's raid the previous day, Wood knew exactly what they were marching into. Taking the abaQulusi completely off guard, by mid-afternoon they had control of the plateau.

From this new position they could see thousands of abaQulusi warriors, as well as some of the followers of the renegade Swazi prince Mbilini waMswati gathered on the slopes of Hlobane four miles to the east. The following morning as No.4 Column

ABOVE · *This photograph in the 1910 travelogue* Storm and Sunshine in South Africa *by Rosamund Southey shows one of the many savage cliff faces that gave Hlobane Mountain its fearsome reputation.*

fought to clear the approach, an exhausted rider presented himself to the colonel and handed over a note from the garrison at Helpmekaar: Isandlwana had fallen.

With No.3 Column in full retreat, No.4 Column was exposed on the right flank as well as contending with the abaQulusi on the left. They decided to move back to the border with the Disputed Territory and dug in on Kambula Hill, "Which," Wood recalled, "I anticipate being able to hold even against the whole Zulu army."

On January 28 a message arrived from Chelmsford directly. Like that sent to Pearson, it advised Wood that "he had a free hand to go anywhere or adopt any measures he might think best," ending: "You must now be prepared to have

Colonel Redvers Buller (pronounced 'Reevers') and men of the Frontier Light Horse keep the enemy at bay to cover the retreat.

> ## "THE ABAQULUSI WERE BRUISED BY THE DEFEAT AT ZUNGWINI AND THE CONSTANT HARASSMENT OF BULLER'S CAVALRY ("THE FRONTIER LIGHT HORSE UNDER COL. BULLER HAS ALL THE FUN," WROTE ONE INFANTRY OFFICER SULLENLY TO HIS SISTER)..."

the whole of the Zulu army on your hands any day."

BAD NEIGHBOURS

The abaQulusi were bruised by the defeat at Zungwini and the constant harassment of Buller's cavalry ("The Frontier Light Horse under Col. Buller has all the fun," wrote one infantry officer sullenly to his sister), but the Zulu do not fight defensive campaigns.

Mbilini rallied local abaQulusi to raid the farms and kraals around the German-Boer town of Lüneburg, slaughtering hundreds of the black labourers and their families, and stealing livestock. Meanwhile, Colonel Wood's policy of coercion had chalked up a victory as Hamu kaMpande, the Zulu king's elder sibling, switched his tribe's allegiance to the British. Cynically, many of them had wet their spears at Isandlwana, but Hamu was always mindful of an opportunity to take his half-brother's place.

Keen to raise the spirits of the besieged

No.1 Column at Eshowe and draw the 20,000-strong army of Cetshwayo to the northwest, Chelmsford wrote to Wood imploring him to conduct an offensive at the end of March. Against his better judgement, Wood planned a two-pronged assault for his colonial cavalry on Hlobane for March 28.

His intelligence was patchy. Estimates as to the number of defenders in the abaQulusi fortress ranged from 1,000 to 4,000, and although it was only 1,500 feet high it was encased in jagged terraces, caves, cliffs and thorny scrub, only accessible via narrow footpaths. Hlobane was divided into two plateaus running east to west, a lower one a mile long and half a mile wide and connected to it by a steep path and a higher one two miles long and a mile and half wide. To the east the forbidding Ityenka Nek connected Hlobane Mountain to Ityentika Mountain, while to the west the lower Zungwini Nek joined it to the plateau taken earlier. Embedded in this mountain chain, a more formidable natural citadel than Hlobane is tough to imagine.

Buller and his 156-strong Frontier Light Horse, supported by a mounted battalion of Wood's Irregulars, a single Royal Artillery rocket, and some fresh colonial units would ascend the east face of Hlobane for the higher plateau, while the recently arrived Lieutenant Colonel Cecil Russell and the other battalion of auxiliaries, would climb from the west to the lower plateau. Russell was regarded as incompetent by Wood and his men were a mix of the despondent remnant of No.3 Column's colonial cavalry and some reserves from elsewhere.

Wood knew that the Zulu army was already on its way to confront the only column still at large in Zululand. What he didn't realise was just how close they were and that they had planned to rendezvous with the abaQulusi at the foot of Hlobane on that same morning.

An already hasty plan was about to become a catastrophe.

FIGHTING UPHILL

Setting off on the morning of March 27, Buller's force of 700 marched south of Hlobane. In an echo of the Zulu feint at Isandlwana, they lit campfires to give the impression they were launching another expedition into Zululand and then crept six miles northeast to bivouac at the foot of Ityenka Nek. As they rode through the night they became separated from the 50-man Border Horse, led by the unreliable Lieutenant Colonel Frederick Weatherley.

The Border Horse were raised from the British community in Transvaal at Weatherley's own expense and included his two sons (one of them only 14 years old). A flamboyant colonial adventurer who served in an Austrian cavalry regiment before fighting with the 6th (Inniskilling) Dragoons in the Indian Mutiny, he was little liked by his more reserved peers.

Russell's force set off later in the day and camped five miles to the west of Hlobane. Wood joined them and conferred with Piet Uys and Captain Charles Potter of Wood's Irregulars, who both had first-hand experience of the mountain.

Wood recalled: "I asked whether, should we have the bad luck after taking the mountain to see Cetshwayo's army advancing, we could get down on the north side, and Mr Potter assured me that we could, by leading our horses. Piet Uys was confident that Colonel Buller would get up, without serious loss, and we agreed that, except in the probable contingency of the Zulu main army coming in sight, our operation ought to be a success."

Their advance wrapped in the early morning mist, Buller's force crept up Ityenka Nek and turned east towards the plateau. They were almost 100 yards from the summit before the abaQulusi sentries opened fire. As easily as the old Uys had predicted, Buller secured the upper plateau but the sheer size of it shocked him, as did the perilous inclines of the track down the southwestern side to the lower plateau, later named 'Devil's Pass', and the route they had taken over Ityenka Nek (neck in English) on the northeastern side. According to Buller, they were "paths such as no man in cold blood would try to get a horse down."

Russell had taken the lower plateau just as easily, but despite being ordered to do so was leery of joining Buller when he saw the cruel climb of Devil's Pass. Instead, he dispatched men to collect the abaQulusi cattle from the southern slopes of Hlobane.

THE TIPPING POINT

Wood, meanwhile, had ridden out with a small escort of Mounted Infantry (made up of men from the 90th Regiment)

❧ THE EXTRAORDINARY PIET UYS

At the start of the Anglo-Zulu War, Colonel Evelyn Wood had been hoping to gather irregular companies of Transvaal Boers to join No.1 Column. Thanks to the high-handed administration of Sir Theophilus Shepstone, Afrikaner resentment to the British presence had risen to such levels that the clear majority had no interest in joining their new newest enemies to wage war on their oldest.

The exception was 52-year old Piet Uys, often called Piet Hlobane to distinguish him from his father with the same name - a leading Voortrekker killed fighting King Dingane kaSenzangakhona at the Battle of Italeni (1838). With 40 mounted Boers, including his four sons and some of his brothers, Uys joined No.1 Column and despite his instinctive distrust of the British developed a relationship of mutual respect with Wood.

On the eve of the Battle of Hlobane, Uys turned to Wood and said: "Colonel, if you are killed I will take care of your children, and if I am killed you will do the same for me." The English aristocrat didn't exactly need the support of the settler-farmer in providing for his family,

Piet Uys at the head of his volunteer unit. Raised in Transvaal from the age of nine, Uys had been fighting the Zulu for most of his life.

but nonetheless Wood solemnly agreed. Colonel Wood honoured his commitment to look after Uys's family and petitioned for them to be granted 36,000 acres of government land.

Lieutenant Colonel Buller, not known for empty words, paid tribute to Uys, writing: "One so courageous and so sagacious I shall never see again. We had better spare 100 men."

to join Buller and bumped into the Border Horse heading in the opposite direction. Raising an eyebrow at Weatherley's excuses (Buller's men could clearly be seen on the plateau above them), Wood ordered him up the mountain where, to the colonel's disgust, the Border Horse immediately took cover among the rocks to escape the scattered fire from the slope. Despite his determination, even the indefatigable Wood was driven to shelter in a stone kraal 200 yards further up the track when abaQulusi hidden in a cave shot his horse and interpreter, Llewellyn Lloyd.

An irregular officer slashes at a meticulously detailed Zulu warrior, an illustration from Bertram Mitford's 1896 work of fiction, The Expiation of Wynne Palliser. Today he is a little remembered writer of colonial adventure, but Mitford was a resident of southern Africa from 1874 and it lent his novels a unique reality.

ABOVE · *Sir Evelyn Wood in 1906, by the end of his career he had reached the rank of field marshal, retiring in 1904.*

Buller had taken the open plateau so suddenly that rather than stand and fight, the abaQulusi had melted into the crevices further down the mountain where they could close the path. Wood's staff officer (and second son of the Earl of Cawdor) Captain the Honourable Ronald Campbell, Coldstream Guards was sent down the track to order Weatherley to bring his men up and clear the cave from where the snipers were keeping Wood and his escort penned in the kraal.

Campbell repeated his order three times before yelling in disgust: "Damn him! He's a coward, I'll turn them out!" Charging towards the gunfire, he was joined by the junior staff officer Lieutenant Henry Lysons, 2nd Battalion, 26th (The Cameronians) Regiment and four men of the escort. Making it to the cave unscathed, Campbell stepped into the gloom and was killed instantly, shot in the head at point blank range by the abaQulusi lurking in the darkness. Leaping over Campbell's body, Lysons and the escort killed the sniper and drove the other warrior out. Buller's men, having seen Wood's

predicament had by this time driven the abaQulusi back from the path.

Wood was close with Lloyd and Campbell. The suddenness of both their deaths shook the characteristically steady hand of his command and his priorities briefly slipped from view. He recovered Campbell's personal possessions and ordered both men immediately buried, reading an abridged version of the field burial service over their graves.

Without the support of Russell on the expansive upper plateau, Buller was beginning to falter. With his men trying to simultaneously consolidate their gains and suppress the abaQulusi menacing the eastern approach, Buller was unable to prevent the abaQulusi regrouping and the fight was steadily growing in intensity.

Buller's attention was suddenly drawn to the sight of a 20,000-strong Zulu army marching in five enormous columns towards Hlobane from the east. He ordered his second in command, Captain Robert 'Bobby' Barton, Coldstream Guards and 30 of the Frontier Light Horse down the approach to gather up the dead and then turn onto the 'right' of the mountain.

He meant the 'right' as they came in on

the eastern approach - onto the terrace of Ityenka Nek and down around north side of the mountain, but Barton thought he meant the 'right' facing down the path. Gathering up Weatherley's stragglers as he went, Barton galloped down to the southern base of the mountain and right into the oncoming Zulu. "Alas for the use of careless words," rued Buller later.

With a massive Zulu force bearing down on them from the east and threatening to flank them from the south, Barton and Weatherley swung northeast to climb up and over the Ityenka Nek. The rocks ahead were spotted with abaQulusi but it was a choice between certain death and probable death, and panicked irregulars flung themselves up the treacherous slope under the incessant crossfire of the Zulu and abaQulusi. Many simply tumbled to their deaths as the rocks slipped out from beneath their hooves, some were slaughtered by their pursuers, and at least one trooper turned his carbine on himself.

Weatherley and his teenage son were killed, while Barton and two dozen others made it over to the north side, but Barton's escape was soon cut short. Another officer had been separated from his horse, so Barton pulled him up into his saddle and the combined weight on his already wounded horse slowed them enough for the Zulu to run them down while their comrades galloped on.

With the Devil at Their Backs

Wood, by this time having followed a track southwest down towards Zungwini, ordered Russell down from the lower plateau to cover Buller's retreat on the neck between Hlobane and Zungwini. Instead, Russell took his 200 men six miles away to the west of Zungwini, on the Kambula side. In his defence, Zungwini Nek was a gentle slope several miles across, compared to the more pronounced Ityenka Nek and he later claimed not to have understood what Wood had been referring to.

On the upper plateau Buller made for the Devil's Pass. He formed up a rearguard of his trusted Frontier Light Horse to hold the abaQulusi back as the men made their halting, uneasy descent on foot to the lower plateau leading their horses by the reins. A few minutes later chaos erupted as the first of the Zulu burst onto the upper plateau to join the abaQulusi.

Buller recalled: "We had to get down the frightful path under a constant and ever-increasing fire, but we should have done tolerably and safely I believe had not my stupid rearguard ceased firing, mistaking Zulus for friends. In a moment Zulus were among us in the rocks. How I got down I shall never know."

Captain Cecil D'arcy of the Frontier Light Horse first became aware that the rearguard had failed when a boulder swept the legs out from under his mount. He described the scene: "I looked up and saw the Zulus right in among the white men, stabbing horses and men. I made a jump and got down somehow or other and ran as hard as I could with 70 rounds of ball cartridge, carbine, a revolver, field-glass and heavy boots."

Buller formed up the Frontier Light Horse - many of whom had lost their mounts - in the chaos at the bottom of the Devil's Pass and made a painfully slow fighting retreat to Zungwini, pursued by abaQulusi and Zulu. Buller desperately trying to save every man he could, personally riding back up the path three times to gather stragglers. For this action he was awarded the Victoria

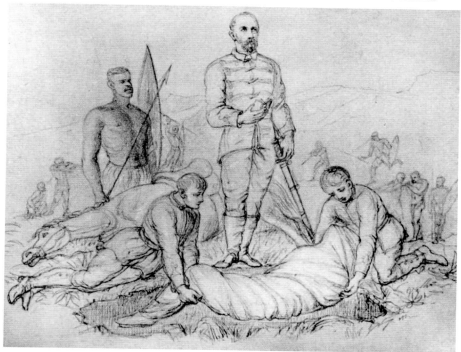

ABOVE · *A bizarre illustration from Wood's 1906 memoir,* From Midshipman to Field Marshal, *depicting the burial of Captain the Honourable Ronald Campbell and Llewellyn Lloyd in the heat of battle.*

Cross, one of six recommendations made following the battle.

Twelve officers and 80 other ranks had been lost, along with over 100 of Wood's Irregulars who had been caught by the Zulu driving the captured cattle north. Piet Uys and his four sons were killed in the descent through Devil's Pass (Uys made it to the bottom of the pass but returned to help one of his sons), and his Boer irregulars deserted during the night. The Frontier Light Horse had suffered so heavily that they were totally ineffective, and the Border Horse no longer existed as a unit. The battered survivors stayed on Zungwini, watching the distant hills, until dusk and then rode for camp under the cover of darkness.

Finally reunited with Russell who protested that he had been given no orders to wait, Buller unleashed his fury: "Perhaps not, but you had no orders to abandon me."

On the morning of March 29, the Zulu began bearing down on Kambula.

In one of the three rescues that saw Colonel Buller awarded his Victoria Cross, he rides back to Devil's Pass to collect stragglers in danger of being run down by the pursuing Zulu.

NO QUARTER, BOYS

The Battle of Kambula, March 29, 1879

There was every reason to expect danger as No.4 Column woke to an ominous blanket of mist. By night, the bruised survivors of the Battle of Hlobane had limped into the hilltop camp lighter by 200 dead and the desertion of many of the black and Boer troops. Brevet Colonel Evelyn Wood, VC, CB hadn't slept much, if at all, and he had checked on the sentries twice in the night.

Cautiously, Wood dispatched two companies of men to cut down trees for the cooking fires (he had made a fetish of supplying his men with fresh bread, by no means the worst vice in the history of the British Army). He reasoned that both morale and energy for the long day ahead would be improved with a hot meal. By way of an early warning, Commandant Pieter Raaff and 20 of his Transvaal Rangers retraced their flight from Zungwini to take in the view from the plateau.

Bringing new meaning to 'irregulars', the Transvaal Rangers were drawn from both white European and black African (predominantly Khoikhoi) labourers in the mining boom town of Kimberley. One officer of the more prestigious Frontier Light Horse recalled his first sight of them, saying: "A more forbidding lot of mixed [Africans] and the scum of the diamond fields was never collected together outside a prison wall."

At around 10am the mist was burnt away by the morning sun and Raaff's outriders raced back to report that the Zulu were camped on the banks of the White Umfolozi River two miles south of Zungwini. Wood's focus on bringing round local chieftains

A company of 1/13th (1st Somersetshire) (Prince Albert's Light Infantry) Regiment of Foot fire over the ridge at the Zulu gathering in the ravine, streaming past the cattle kraal. The main laager can be seen in the left of the illustration, and the booming guns of Fort Kambula in the middle.

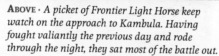

ABOVE · *A picket of Frontier Light Horse keep watch on the approach to Kambula. Having fought valiantly the previous day and rode through the night, they sat most of the battle out.*

ABOVE RIGHT · *Commandant Pieter Edward Raaff pictured after the Anglo-Zulu War, following his appointment as a Companion of the Order of St Michael and St George (CMG) in recognition of the role played by the Transvaal Rangers in the conflict. Buller described him as: "A perfect type of a border soldier, brave, indefatigable, and deeply versed in African warfare."*

had yielded a complete report on the enemy composition from a Zulu who wandered away from the column and hadn't reckoned on his host's shifting allegiances.

At 11am the Zulu were on the move.

MEETING THE STORM

As soon as No.4 Column had arrived at Kambula they began laagering their wagons and entrenching them with all the ingenuity the Royal Engineers could muster.

Like the prow of a ship, two 7-pounders were installed in a narrow knoll to the east with a company of 90th Regiment of Foot (Perthshire Volunteers) and a company and a half of 1/13th (1st Somersetshire) (Prince Albert's Light Infantry) Regiment of Foot. This, Fort Kambula, was a redoubt of steep earth banks and the pivot of the defence.

Adjoining the southwest corner of Fort Kambula by way of a five-foot wooden palisade was a kraal made from laagered wagons that sheltered a company of the 13th and the column's 2,000 cattle. This pushed right up to the edge of a ridge that obscured the defenders' field of fire. The kraal would offer a tempting target for

Zulu infiltrators, but it would be effectively luring them into the crossfire between two entrenched positions.

Wood recalled wryly: "To those who objected that the Zulus would charge and knock [the palisade] down by the weight of their bodies, I replied it would cause a delay of several minutes during which 300 or 400 rifles, at 250 yards' range, ought to make an additional barricade of human bodies."

The main laager was 300 yards west of Fort Kambula. The wagons were drawn into a hexagon, their wheels chained so they couldn't be moved, and the spaces between the wagon and the ground packed with earth. Mealie bags were stacked along the top rails (where the canvas tent meets the wooden sides of the wagon), transforming them into raised firing platforms. Ditches were dug in front of the laager, both as a firing position and to increase the height of the laager itself against the Zulu charge.

Defending the main laager was the bulk of the 90th and 1/13th, over 600 assorted cavalrymen with their Martini-Henry carbines, the 58 of Wood's Irregulars who hadn't deserted the night before, 11 Royal Engineers, and those men of the Royal Artillery who weren't required by the gun crews. Ammunition boxes were opened and placed behind the firing line.

With their rear covered by the men in the two laagers, the four remaining 7-pounders were positioned on the open hillside between the two fieldworks, facing northeast - a gentle slope in which Wood ordered range markers of white stone placed at appropriate intervals.

THE HOSPITAL ON THE FRONTIER

Their bleeding staunched at the front, those who could be stabilised were dispatched by mule-drawn ambulance 20 miles to Utrecht, Transvaal. There, the Army Medical Department (consisting of both military and civilian personnel, volunteer nurses and black orderlies) ran a base field hospital that took the wounded from Intombe, Hlobane and Kambula.

A purpose-built collection of huts constructed from wattle and clay, the base field hospital at Utrecht was built with 150 patients in mind but outbreaks of enteric fever and two battles in two days pushed them well beyond capacity. In April 1879 alone, 50 men from the 250-strong garrison at Utrecht were hospitalised with what the *Sunderland Daily Echo and Shipping Gazette* described as, "a very severe type of intermittent fever, said to have arisen from rotting commissariat stores at Rorke's Drift."

At Helpmekaar - swollen with the wounded from the Battle of Isandlwana - long biscuit boxes were covered in sackcloth by way of additional bedding. A similar solution can be imagined at Utrecht. A separate officer's hospital was established in a local house, hired from its occupants.

The base field hospital was run by Surgeon-Major Charles Cuffe, Army Hospital Corps, in his role as Principal

The wounded of the Battle of Hlobane finally arrive in Utrecht, Transvaal by ambulance. Their destination was the increasingly overcrowded base field hospital in the town.

Medical Officer for the northern campaign, and he took in Zulu wounded as well as British and colonials. This alone is evidence that despite the horrendous lapses in decency from the men at the front, not all defeated or fallen Zulu were butchered. Cuffe wrote to *The Times* newspaper that, "The prisoners themselves wondered at this kindness and frequently told us that had our wounded fallen into their hands they would have assegaied them without mercy.

On October 30, 1879 *The Telegraph* described "six Zulu prisoners, wounded at the Battle of Kambula, who have been here ever since March. Hitherto, they have had a surgeon in attendance who spoke their language, but now they are under the charge of a kind-hearted orderly [...] They are all badly wounded, and three, at least, should have their legs amputated, but they will not submit to an operation, and the result is not doubtful."

Calmly, the men of Kambula ate their lunch, collapsed their tents and retired to their positions.

TAUNTING THE BULL

The five great columns of the Zulu army appeared on the horizon to the southeast and the British watched them form up into the Horns of the Buffalo. The left horn peeled away to the south of the camp, the chest climbed the eastern edge of the ridge, and the right horn looped around to the gentle slopes of the northern side of Kambula Hill.

Mnyamana kaNgqengelele, chief minister to the Zulu King Cetshwayo kaMpande and head of the Buthelezi tribe, was not a rash man. The decision to target Lord Chelmsford's No.2 Column was his and he shared command with Chief Ntshingwayo kaMahole, the 70-year old victor of Isandlwana whose feints had divided the British force into two bite-sized morsels.

Both of them knew better than to pile onto a fortified position, as the King's half-brother had done so

calamitously at Rorke's Drift, but like the regiments at Rorke's Drift, the warriors were hungry for battle. Flushed with their success of the day before, even two of Zululand's most capable field commanders would struggle to contain their energies.

At 1.30pm, as the Zulu moved into position, Lieutenant Colonel Redvers Buller suggested that he take the Mounted Infantry (rather than his cherished Frontier Light Horse) and see if he could goad part of the right horn into prematurely charging. Aside from the troopers who had served as Wood's escort, the Mounted Infantry hadn't taken part in the Battle of Hlobane and both men and mounts were rested. Wood agreed, one of the laager's wagons was rolled aside, and the men galloped down the slope. Dismounting, they formed a skirmish line and unleashed a volley of rifle fire into the flanks of the iNgobamakhosi regiment, pulling back they repeated the feat taunting the iButho with the crack of their carbines.

Buller recalled: "They did not stand our attack as I pressed home, and the advance

of their right column, about 2,000 strong, turned and charged us. I need not tell you that the 80 or 90 men I had got on their horses pretty quick, and we scampered back to camp holding a running fight with them as we went."

At 300 yards, the guns of the 90th Regiment opened up from the main laager and the rifles of the redoubt joined in. In their shadow came the boom of Royal Artillery shrapnel shells that peppered the iNgobamakhosi with 63 bullets in each shot.

Whatever lessons might be taught by this cautionary tale was already lost on the Zulu. Fierce rivalries between amaButho boiled over when the iNgobamakhosi broke, and the others followed so not to allow their peers glory at their own regiment's expense. By 2.30pm the whole Zulu iMpi was tearing across the grass of the Kambula Hill towards the barricades.

SHOT AND SHELL

As the right horn streamed up the northeasterly slope, the chest and the left horn emerged over the crest of the ravine on the opposite side of the laager, the concealment taking them to within 100 yards of the defenders before they were cut down.

The initial bloodlust abating, 40 Zulu with rifles snuck into the tall mealie around a rubbish heap to the west. Occupying this spot of high ground concealed from the laager itself but exposed to the southern edge of the hill, they caught a company of the 13th Regiment unawares. Wood ordered them in closer to the laager, where they were safely out of the enemy's line of sight.

As a bullet struck one soldier in the leg, Wood instinctively darted forward to help him and was stopped by his staff officer (replacing Wood's beloved friend, the late Captain the Honourable Ronald Campbell). Captain Maud reproached his commander, saying: "Really, sir, it isn't your place to pick up single men." Maud grabbed two lieutenants and went out himself.

With the withdrawing men unable to cover the cattle kraal as effectively from their new firing line, the Zulu managed to drive the defenders from the stockade in a vicious close quarter scrap among the panicked cattle. From there they were able to fire on the unprotected rear of the four 7-pounders.

Commanding two of the four guns with Lieutenant Arthur Bigge taking the other pair, Lieutenant Frederick Slade wrote home: "On came the Zulu in their thousands and by 3.30pm had actually driven our infantry out of and had occupied the cattle laager which was only 40 yards from my guns. I fired round after round of case [canisters packed with lead balls, used at close range] into them, hitting oxen and Zulus alike, and a merry hell of bullets were pouring into us."

The artillery fire grew so intense that the breeches had to be cooled with water before shells could be loaded, and with no breeze, the air around them was thick with smoke and the stench of gunpowder. Wood was fulsome in his praise of the artillery officers (Slade and Bigge were "unsurpassable"), but especially Lieutenant Frederick Nicholson who commanded the two guns in Fort Kambula:

"The men belonged to garrison companies, but I have never known a

LEFT · *A simplified plan of the battle showing the layout of Kambula Hill, the fort, the palisade, the cattle kraal and the main laager.*

A laager being entrenched with earth banks and mealie bags, while trenches in front act as a firing line for the defenders. The fieldworks that Wood threw up at Kambula would not have been dissimilar.

A skirmish line of Mounted Infantry, wearing bandoliers and wielding Martini-Henry carbines open fire on the Zulu, their horses wait behind them for a quick retreat.

battery so exceptionally fortunate in its subalterns. Lieutenant Nicholson, standing on the gun platform, fought his guns with the unmoved stoical courage habitual to his nature."

TWISTING THE BAYONET

As the Zulu will to fight began to ebb, Wood spotted warriors gathering on a terrace in the ravine just below the kraal, their leaders desperately trying to urge them up the steep hillside. Wood ordered two companies of the 90th under Brevet Major Robert Hackett to fix bayonets and drive the hesitant Zulu over the crest of their rocky terrace and send them scattering into the ravine below.

Spotting an iNduna waving a red flag to direct them, the colonel brought up a Martini-Henry carbine he'd borrowed from a cavalryman, but the barrel was so hot from the incessant rate of fire that he fired while it was still aimed at the Zulu's feet. The ricochet struck him in the stomach and when another two chiefs picked up the banner, Wood repeated the feat by aiming low and letting the recoil find its target.

Hackett's advance sent the warriors cowering in the ravine in full retreat, but in straying too far from the covering fire of the laager, they found themselves caught in the crossfire from the sharpshooters in the mealie to the west. Twenty-five men were killed or wounded as they withdrew;

21-year-old Lieutenant Arthur Bright was shot clean through one thigh, the splash of gore so thick that the medics missed the fact that it had shattered the other thigh bone, and Hackett was shot through the temple, the bullet passing right through his head. Bright died later that night, while Hackett implausibly survived.

Having sat out the worst of it, the momentum of the Zulu army was beginning to crumble with every bold counterattack from the defenders. Lieutenant Colonel Buller had seen off a part of the Zulu left horn with a bayonet charge from some of the 1/13th, his action taking place simultaneously with Hackett's, it was enough to take the whole left flank

7-pounders from Zulu who had got in among the crews while his mind was fixed on victory.

The attacks were now coming in fits and starts. All hope of a Zulu victory was long gone, and at 5.15pm, Wood ordered Slade and two companies of 1/13th to clear the kraal which they did successfully this time. Finally, Wood led another raid on the ravine chasing away the dregs of the assault.

Wood marvelled: "The line battalions were very steady, expending in four hours an average 33 rounds a man; though that evening I heard that some of them had thought the possibility of resisting such overwhelming numbers of brave savages, 13 or 14 to one man, was more than doubtful."

RUN THEM DOWN

With the Zulu in retreat, the mounted irregulars saddled their horses and rode from the laager to give chase. This was their reckoning for the humiliation

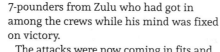

of the Zulu out of the fight.

Meanwhile, the artillerymen holding firm by their guns in the nek between Fort Kambula and the laager could see the wind had been knocked from the chest of the Zulu. Weary of the steady whistle of bullets from the Zulu to his rear, Lieutenant Slade drew his sword and led some of his men to retake the cattle kraal. It was an ill-advised adventure. Slade was forced to pull his men back to defend the

ABOVE · *Lieutenant Frederick Nicholson, Royal Artillery. When he fell, his place in Fort Kambula was taken by the RA Director of Transport, Major Vaughn.*

LEFT · *Lieutenant-Colonel Redvers Buller, pictured after 1885 with the rank of major-general. Following the Anglo-Zulu War, Buller served as Wood's chief of staff in the First Boer War (1880-1881) and his head of intelligence in the Anglo-Egyptian War (1882). Buller earned this promotion leading an infantry brigade in Sudan in 1884.*

of Hlobane and it was only the fading light and the sheer exhaustion from two days of combat that prevented a massacre. "We were up and at them," recalled Buller. "Had it not been dark their loss would have been very heavy."

Captain Cecil D'Arcy, Buller's second-in-command of the Frontier Light Horse, left nothing to the imagination in his account: "[We] followed them for eight miles, butchering the brutes all over the place. I told the men: 'No quarter boys, remember yesterday'."

The number of Zulu dead was staggering. "In the next few days we buried 785 men within 300 yards of our laager," said Wood, "which we were afterwards obliged to shift on account of the number of bodies which lay unseen in the hollows."

Wood's concern turned to the wounded and he was deeply affected by the plight of Major Robert Hackett, whose charge had helped turn the tide of the battle: "He was a piteous sight, for a bullet had passed from one temple to another, and, without actually hitting the eyes, had protruded the eyeballs, injuring the brain. He was unconscious of the terrible nature of his wounds, possibly from pressure on the brain, and observed to me, 'Your Commissariat officers are very stingy in not lighting up this hospital tent; the place is in absolute darkness'."

The hospital tents in the laager, already heaving with the wounded of Hlobane, were a hive of activity throughout the wet and rainy night. Twenty-nine men lay dead or dying - including Lieutenant Nicholson, Royal Artillery who had finally paid the price for standing astride the parapet of Fort Kambula directing his shells - and another 55 were wounded.

In the wake of Kambula, the Zulu army - many of the warriors having fought at Isandlwana, Hlobane and now Kambula - scattered hungry and demoralised, with the men returning to their home kraals. King Cetshwayo was furious with his two senior commanders, but no amount of screaming or shouting could now change the fate of the Zulu Kingdom.

Never again in the Anglo-Zulu War would the Zulu be able to muster truly overwhelming numbers against the invader. If they had squandered their early victories, Lord Chelmsford and his commanders hadn't ignored the bitter lessons of their early defeats. From now on, the British would fight defensively, bringing their awesome firepower to bear where it could be concentrated, and they would put a greater emphasis on intelligence gathering and reconnaissance.

WHAT IS TO BE DONE?

The Second Invasion of Zululand

Cape Colony governor Sir Henry Bartle Frere's plan to present victory to the Colonial Office as a fait accompli was sunk. He had started a war and Lord Chelmsford was losing it.

Lord Chelmsford, doing a fair bit of blame-shifting and misdirection, reported the defeat at Isandlwana to the War Office in brief terms. The general's telegram arrived in the morning of February 11, 1879. In it he asked for at least three infantry battalions, two cavalry regiments, and a company of Royal Engineers to reinforce the battered columns of the initial invasion.

Despite the best intentions of the British government to avoid another costly entanglement in Africa, Frere and Chelmsford had committed them and they needed to win. The British public, who cared little for the budget and didn't even

know they had been at war with the Zulu until February, had been galvanised by the drama of the defeat at Isandlwana and the defiance of Rorke's Drift. The cabinet decided to provide Chelmsford with the reinforcements he requested and double the number of infantry battalions to six.

TREADING CAREFULLY

Unaware of exactly what the situation was, the government made sure to support the war effort in public, but behind closed doors knives were being sharpened. The Prime Minister, Benjamin Disraeli, was livid. He had urged restraint and the men in the field had done the exact opposite. Spending weeks alternating between deep depression and fury, he suggested to Queen Victoria that Lord Chelmsford was to blame.

For once, the monarch and her favourite were at loggerheads. Victoria had a great personal bond with the army and she ordered a telegram dispatched to Chelmsford letting him know that she "sympathises most sincerely with him in the dreadful loss which has deprived her of so many gallant officers and men." She instructed the Colonial Secretary, Michael Hicks Beach, to send a similar message to Frere, much to the irritation of the cabinet and the no doubt deepening misery of the Prime Minister.

Horse Guards, the Westminster headquarters of the British Army, had its own opinions. Two memoranda - one signed by three senior generals, and the other produced by the Intelligence Department - circulated on February 11 offering cutting assessments of Chelmsford's lack of reconnaissance, lack

BELOW · *The 1864 dress uniform of the Argyllshire Highlanders private, officer and piper. It was only from 1863 that the 91st began to style themselves as a Highland regiment, but the War Office drew the line at allowing a kilt for all ranks.*

In high spirits, the Highlanders wave Britain goodbye as they sail for Durban.

land at Durban. Chelmsford immediately pressed them into action for the relief of Eshowe, hoping to uncage the fighting men of Colonel Charles Pearson's No.4 Column.

The earliest arrivals were 9th Duke of Edinburgh's (Lanarkshire) Regiment of Foot, 57th (West Middlesex) Regiment of Foot, 3rd Battalion of the 60th (The King's Royal Rifle Corps), and 91st (Princess Louise's Argyllshire Highlanders) Regiment of Foot. The fetching rifle green tunics of the 3rd KRRC and the Black Watch tartan trews of the Highlanders breaking up the sea of red. Chelmsford raised new companies of Natal Native Contingent, and a new scout force, the Natal Volunteer Guides.

Chelmsford was keen to get a better lay of the land and convinced John

of fortifications, lack of communication, and sheer foolishness in being lured away by a Zulu feint. Four major generals were to be attached to the reinforcements, one to act as Chelmsford's deputy and another to organise his lines of communication. He wasn't being punished just yet, but the reins were tightening.

ABOVE · *19 officers and two boys of the 57th (West Middlesex) Regiment of Foot pose in front of a regimental hut, 1864.*

Victoria's private secretary, Sir Edward Ponsonby, captured the mood, saying: "The evil is done. To punish [Frere] for that by withdrawing him would be to punish ourselves, for it is against Abraham Lincoln's dictum that it is unwise to swap horses while crossing a stream."

For a while, Horse Guards took the same attitude with Chelmsford and in return, he dropped his rolling campaign of blaming his subordinates (first the late Lieutenant Colonel Arthur Durnford, and then Colonel Richard Glyn) for the defeat at Isandlwana. Only when the scale of his misjudgements became clear in April, did the mood of the military establishment turn firmly against him.

What Chelmsford and Frere kept to themselves was that the Zulu king had already reached out in the wake of Isandlwana and Rorke's Drift to sue for peace, but their war was now endangering their careers and not just lives. Only the total defeat of the Zulu would suffice to safeguard the men at the top.

THE NEW WAR

Starting in March and continuing into April 1879, reinforcements began to

Robert Dunn, the 'white iNduna', to become his head of intelligence. The Africa-born settler was close friend and advisor to the Zulu King Cetshwayo, who had given him several kraals to rule as chief. He had tried to remain neutral, but now Dunn could see which way the wind was blowing and decided to throw in with Zululand's new management.

Following the Siege of Eshowe, Chelmsford reorganised his force again dividing them into the First Division (or Coastal Column) which consisted of the relief column, plus Pearson's No.4 Column, and the Second Division which would follow the route of the luckless No.3 Column (albeit staying well clear of the corpse-covered ground of Isandlwana). This was composed entirely of troops newly arrived from Britain.

As the only original column still fighting fit, Chelmsford was reluctant to interrupt Brevet Colonel Evelyn Wood's winning formula of aggressive raiding and tribal subversion. Giving him the brevet rank of brigadier general, his column was designated a flying column and ordered to support the Second Division. ◄◄

ABOVE · *A private and an officer of the King's Royal Rifle Corps in marching order rifle green tunics and shakos.*

CLINGING TO POWER

As more detail filtered through from the front, Chelmsford's limitations had become obvious. The calls for the general to be replaced steadily grew to include Frere, the architect of the war. Hicks Beach echoed the governor's own cynical sentiments months earlier, saying: "Had all gone successfully, comparatively few would have blamed you."

Frere narrowly escaped recall to London but was publicly chastised. He would remain at his post just long enough to start the First Boer War (1880-1881), another needless campaign in the shotgun wedding of South Africa.

THE TRAP IS SPRUNG

The Battle of Gingindlovu, April 2, 1879

Brevet Major Percy Barrow's Mounted Infantry give chase at the end of the Battle of Gingindlovu. The toughened cattle hide shields of the Zulu turned out to be effective at turning away cavalry sabres.

O n March 29, the same day that Brevet Colonel Evelyn Wood's No.4 Column was seeing off the bulk of the Zulu army at Kambula, Lord Chelmsford's relief column crossed the Lower Drift over the River Tugela. Behind them lay Fort Pearson, a reminder of the commander they were going to save.

Chelmsford's new column was the largest ever assembled in Zululand. It was built around four battalions of line infantry - three complete battalions of the new arrivals (57th West Middlesex, 91st Argyllshire Highlanders, and 3/60th King's Royal Rifle Corps) and four companies each from the 2/3rd (The Buffs) Regiment of Foot and 99th (Lanarkshire) Regiment of Foot.

The relief column was supported by a Naval Brigade of 170 sailors and a company of Royal Marine Light Infantry, an artillery battery of two 9-pounder guns,

two Gatling guns and two rocket tubes; two battalions of Natal Native Contingent; 70 mounted irregulars under Brevet Major Percy Barrow, 19th Hussars; and 150 of the 'white iNduna' John Dunn's black levies.

Total strength was over 5,600 combat troops (approximately 3,300 white and 2,300 black) and it dragged behind it a train of over a hundred ox wagons and 44 carts. The wagons were so laden down with supplies - 10 days' worth for his own force and then extras for Pearson's men - that it took 32 draught oxen to pull each one.

This time Chelmsford was taking no chances. He issued strict instructions that each wagon would carry ammunition boxes within easy reach, and that the lids of the regimental reserve boxes should have the screw removed for quick access. Each night they would form a square laager surrounded by a trench - the British and colonials would

bivouac between the trench and the laager, while the auxiliaries, horses and cattle would shelter within. Pickets would be stationed half a mile out from each face of the square to sound the alarm.

Could this have saved the camp at Isandlwana? It would have blessed them with a fighting chance, at least.

Gin-Gin-Love-You

Hugging the open terrain along the coast rather than repeating Pearson's hilly route inland, for the first two days of the march the relief column saw little of the enemy, even when Major Barrow and his men put a few kraals to the torch. Progress was slow, the drifts were deeper from the torrential rains and the men waded through the chest-high water with their rifles and kit bags around their heads and shoulders.

On April 1, the column laagered for the night on a knoll by the Gingindlovu Stream (the rankers pronounced it with some merriment as 'Gin-gin-love-you'). The site was chosen by John Dunn, and Chelmsford's senior aide-de-camp, Captain William Molyneux immediately set about marking up the laager. Each face of the square was 130 yards long and each trench stood 15 yards in front of the laager. Its dimensions were measured so precisely that it could be manned by 2,000 men standing two-deep, leaving over 1,000 for reserves, pickets, and other duties.

Molyneux marvelled: "The distances worked out beautifully; we had guns, rockets, or Gatlings, at the angles of the trench; an opening in the middle of each face to let the horses and cattle in and out, with four wagons ready to run in and close it at any moment."

From the high ground, they could see five miles of rough, swampy terrain and then another nine or ten miles of undulating foothills with long grass. At the end of some 15 miles of ambush country was Fort Eshowe where the heliograph flashed a warning: a sizeable iMpi had entered the Inyezane Valley. As night fell, Dunn and Molyneux rode out in silence to the Inyezane River and saw the campfires of a growing Zulu army.

The Zulu would almost certainly attack early the next day. It was the best-case scenario if they had to fight: they were entrenched, they held the high ground, the way ahead was unfavourable, and the weather was so foul that the wagons would be almost impossible to move by morning.

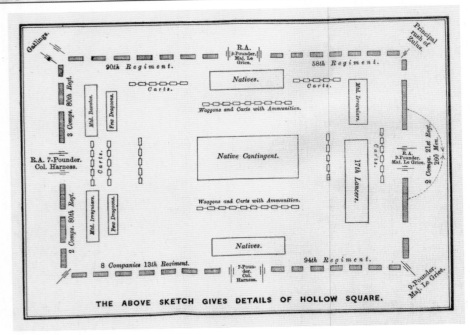

The charge reached 500 yards the rifles of the infantry barked their greeting. "Rockets look awful instruments of destruction," observed Molyneux, "but they do none at all except when used to frighten horses or to set tents on fire. The Zulus evidently thought them living devils, for I saw many men fire at them as they passed over their heads."

Taking the brunt of this first charge, Private WG Ransley of 3/60th recalled: "Soon the Zulus got within 300 yards of our laager, they having crept up under cover afforded by the long grass, clumps of trees and bushes. It was here our fire caused them to fall in heaps."

Green beyond their tunics, this was the first action for many of the 3/60th, including the 22-year-old Lieutenant Arthur Mynors. He wrote: "Our men were awfully frightened and nervous at first, could not even speak and shivered from funk, so we - the officers - had enough to do to keep the men cool."

ABOVE · *A simplified plan of the square at Gingindlovu. The placement of wagons and guns is slightly misleading, however.*

"The trench was completed but full of water in places," wrote Molyneux, "and the state of the ground inside it defies description. When 5,000 human beings, 2,000 oxen and 300 horses have been churning up five acres of very sodden ground for two or three hours, it makes a compost neither pretty to look at, easy to move about in, nor nice to smell. There were unpleasant reptiles about also, for two puff adders had just been killed close to our wagon."

SWIFT AND BOLD

As the dim morning light crept through the low-lying mist, it was followed by the Zulu. "No preparation was necessary," recalled Chelmsford, "and no orders had to be given beyond the saddling up of the horses of the officers of the staff: the troops were already at their posts."

On the north face of the square opposite the Inyezane River, were the 3/60th Rifles, on the east face the 57th West Middlesex, on the west the 99th Lanarkshire and the 2/3rd Buffs, and on the south the 91st Argyllshire Highlanders. The Naval Brigade held each corner with their mountain guns, Gatling guns and rockets.

The iMpi they faced was little more than a hastily assembled rabble made up of 12,000 warriors from coastal tribes and other local levies and supported by the battle-weary remnants of the royal iButho. At the head of the army was Chief Somopho kaZikhala, one of King

ABOVE · *The Natal Native Contingent wait behind the Naval Brigade, seated and ordered to point their rifles upwards to stop them acting prematurely. They were roughly handled by their white officers and struck in the head if they fired in the air.*

Cetshwayo kaMpande's advisors, but the King's impulsive half-brother Dabulamanzi kaMpande was there too. His kraals were just to the west of Eshowe.

Just before 6am, the attack began. As soon as they crossed the river, the iMpi gracefully formed up into their standard configuration: the left horn and chest advancing towards the north face of the laager, and the right horn splitting into two and moving towards the western and southern sides. In the hills beyond Inyezane, the loins lurked watching and waiting.

The Gatlings and the rocket tubes on the northern corners opened up first and when

Lieutenant-Colonel Francis Vernon Northey did more than enough. Spurring on the 3/60th, the 43-year old warhorse directed the Gatling crews and blazed away with his revolver until he was shot in the shoulder. Once his wound had been dressed, he returned to the line and continued to direct the defence slumped against a wagon with blood seeping from his bandages, until he finally passed out. An artery had been severed and he died four days later.

THE GLEEFUL SLAUGHTER

With the left horn falling back, the battle moved to the south and west. NNC Captain

Guy Dawney, firing from behind the Argyllshire Highlanders, recalled: "We kept up heavy fire at every black figure we saw, but they crawled through the grass, and dodged behind bushes, shooting at us all the time, and soon every bush in front of us held and hid two or three Zulu... Our sights came down from 500, 400, 300, 200, to 100 yards; but no Zulu got nearer to the shelter trench than 31 yards."

On the north face, Chelmsford ordered out the cavalry to clear away the remaining Zulu. Straying too far from the cover of the 3/60th, the Mounted Infantry found themselves in danger of being encircled. Molyneux galloped out to bring them back and as he did so his own horse was shot. The dutiful mount just about getting him back to the laager before Molyneux was thrown to the ground.

With Major Barrow returned from his raid, Chelmsford ordered the cavalry down the eastern side of the square and into the

flank of the right horn. At the same time, the Argyllshire Highlanders had knocked the wind from the Zulu assault, and Dawney and the Natal Native Contingent charged from the laager as the anvil to Barrow's hammer.

"The actual number of men killed with the sword were probably few," admitted Barrow, "but the morale effect on the retreating Zulus as the swordsmen closed in on them was very great. In most cases they threw themselves down and showed no fight and were assegaid by the Natal Native Contingent who followed up."

Molyneux recalled the Naval Brigade's commodore and his flag lieutenant joining the slaughter after ordering his men to stay put. The carnival atmosphere is somewhat sadistic in retrospect: "Away they went hacking and slashing on foot, while the tars, who obeyed orders and never stirred yelled with delight.... 'Now you've got 'em! Look out, sir, there's one to the right in the

grass!' til everyone was roaring with laughter."

In just shy of an hour, the Zulu offensive had been broken. The artillery continued to shell the fleeing foe who were run down by the cavalry over miles. The battle had cost the Zulu estimated 1,000 dead to two British and colonial officers and 11 other ranks killed, and four officers and 44 men wounded.

THE RELIEF OF ESHOWE

The next morning, Chelmsford set off to Eshowe with supplies. It was slow going over the swamps with the wagon train and the first man into Fort Eshowe arrived a good hour before the army.

It was Charles Norris-Newman, a war correspondent with the *Standard*, whose arrival was recorded by one of Pearson's staff officers: "'First in Eshowe!' he exclaimed, with a self-satisfied air. 'Proud to shake hands with an Eshowian.'" Five minutes later a disappointed reporter from the *Argus* arrived, having apparently lost the race to become a part of the story.

The garrison erupted into cheers when Major Barrow arrived at 6pm with his Mounted Infantry, and at 8pm Lord Chelmsford marched into Fort Eshowe followed by the wailing pipes of the Argyllshire Highlanders.

On April 4, Dabulamanzi's nearby kraal was set aflame while the prince himself watched sullenly from a distant hill, firing a few token rounds at the British and then disappearing. A small garrison was left at Fort Eshowe, and the rest decamped for Gingindlovu. The coastal road would now take the brunt of the invasion from Natal. 🗡️

BELOW · *The view from within the square as the Argyllshire Highlanders stand two-deep in the shelter trench, while behind them the irregulars fire from the laager.*

Two officers inspect the graves at Gingindlovu. The oversized headstones making clear the names of the fallen for readers of the newspaper.

THE WAR OF THE
GENERALS

The Battle of Ulundi, July 4, 1879

Stunned by the recent defeats, the Zulu King Cetshwayo kaMpande was said to have uttered at the beginning of April 1879 that trying to hold back the British now was as futile as "a man warding off a falling tree."

By mid-May, Lord Chelmsford's forces had been almost completely replenished and the tree had begun to lean towards the Zulu capital, Ulundi. Assigned to the coastal route through Gingindlovu from the south, the veteran First Division was commanded by Major General Henry Hope Crealock, one of the reinforcements and the brother of Chelmsford's widely disliked military secretary, Lieutenant Colonel John North Crealock. On April 21, they crossed the Lower Tugela with instructions to destroy two royal kraals before moving on to Ulundi.

The Second Division, due to enter Zululand from the west, was led by Major General Edward Newdigate, and was accompanied by Chelmsford. They crossed the Blood River at Kopje Alleen on May 31 and staying well north of Isandlwana planned to rejoin the old Rorke's Drift-to-Ulundi road in the Babanango Mountains. They were mostly recent arrivals from Britain and so were shadowed by Brevet Brigadier General Evelyn Wood's hard-fighting Flying Column.

CUTTING CHELMSFORD DOWN TO SIZE

Though Chelmsford was riding high in the aftermath of Kambula and Gingindlovu, back in Britain attitudes towards the general were hardening.

Prince George, Duke of Cambridge and commander-in-chief of the British Army, was increasingly sure that blame for Isandlwana was borne by Chelmsford alone, and he had begun to spot inconsistencies and outright fabrications in his explanations for the disaster. A series of deeply critical letters had also arrived from Major General the Honourable Henry Clifford, VC who had been dispatched with the reinforcements to take charge of Chelmsford's shoddy supply lines.

While Chelmsford and Frere once exploited the weeks-long communication lag to disregard orders they didn't like, now it was working against them. Despite the reversal ⟫⟫

The charge of the 17th (The Duke of Cambridge's Own) Lancers at Ulundi, by the celebrated Victorian military artist Orlando Norie.

of fortunes in the field at Gingindlovu, Chelmsford's bad news from March was still coming down the line.

On April 8, days after the Battle of Kambula and the relief of Eshowe, reports from Hlobane arrived in Britain. Though victories followed almost immediately, the further catastrophic loss of life in southern Africa had done little to relieve the anxiety of British Prime Minister, Benjamin Disraeli. He opined that: "A general of genius might put all right, but I fear he does not exist or is locked up in Cyprus."

High Commissioner of Cyprus since 1878 when it had been ceded to Britain by treaty, Major General Sir Garnet Wolseley seemed like the obvious solution. Two of the most capable commanders already in Zululand - Wood and Buller - were part of his clique, and he had brought the 3rd Anglo-Ashanti War in the Gold Coast to a close in two months.

Disraeli still had the Queen to appease - her support for Chelmsford and Frere was unwavering. He assured her that there was no intention (yet) to undermine the pair, but a strong hand "intimately acquainted with the views and policy of your Majesty's government" might be what was needed to steer the war to a close. While Victoria left for Balmoral, Disraeli launched his policy coup.

He telegrammed her to report that the cabinet believed Sir Garnet Wolseley should be dispatched to southern Africa. As the senior officer, he would naturally take command over Chelmsford. Additionally, he was to be appointed governor of Natal and Transvaal, as well as replacing Frere as High Commissioner. This reduced Chelmsford to second-in-command and bottled Frere up in Cape Colony.

BELOW · *The 88th Regiment of Foot (Connaught Rangers) unload supply wagons. Part of the First Division, they saw little fighting.*

ABOVE · *Major General Edward Newdigate commanded Second Division, but the presence of Lord Chelmsford effectively left him without a role.*

As a constitutional monarch, her responses were limited to her formidable disapproval. She replied: "I will not withhold my sanction though I cannot approve it."

Writing in his journal, Wolseley judged astutely: "How curious and uncomfortable it was that [Disraeli] had not come to this present decision three months ago... If the war is to be finished by August: I shall have to follow the lines laid down by Chelmsford, lines which I believe to be fundamentally wrong."

CREALOCK'S CRAWLERS

Back on the coastal route, Crealock had run into supply problems almost instantly. There simply weren't enough wagons, with most of the available transport

ABOVE · *Major General Henry Hope Crealock, painted by Robert Russ with the rank of lieutenant general and wearing the Order of St Michael and St George. Crealock retired in 1884 and the Anglo-Zulu War was his last action.*

having been requisitioned for the first invasion. Natal was pushing back against Chelmsford's constant demands for support, fearing that if they let the army take any more of their wagons, carts, oxen and teams then the day-to-day business of the colony would collapse.

The First Division's progress was so pitiable that the column was nicknamed 'Crealock's Crawlers'. The rate of sickness among the animals working long hours in hot, damp conditions was taking its toll too, and the men were scarcely better off: enteric fever and dysentery saw huge numbers of troops rotating in and out of the field hospital.

Crealock did manage to partially solve his issue with supply, taking not just two important staging posts - called Fort Crealock and Fort Chelmsford with the traditional modesty of the Victorian major general - but a relatively sheltered beach. Optimistically called Port Durnford, it was a rare stretch of this wild coast that could be landed by the surfboats of the Royal Navy.

As instructed, the two royal kraals - emaNgwani and Hlalangubo - were set alight, although both were deserted. The Zulu army was depleted to the point that it was no longer able to fight on more than one front, and so Cetshwayo had gathered his iMpi around him at the capital. Along the coast, the chiefs ignored the King's call to arms. Many of their young had already been slain and the invader was on their doorstep.

Even the King's family were surrendering. On April 21, Makwendu kaMpande, one of Cetshwayo's many half-brothers, turned himself over to Crealock.

Chopping Wood with a Razor

His progress just as slow and his supply lines just as overwhelmed, Chelmsford set his jaw, confronted his greatest shame, and sent a small force to recover the wagons from the open-air charnel house at Isandlwana. Untouched for months, bodies lay where they fell, and 34 perfectly serviceable wagons were pulled away - only the lack of horses prevented them from taking more.

It was a grim job, the elements had stripped some of the corpses to bone while others were desiccated by the hot sun, their parched features still chillingly recognisable as the men they had once been. Papers were recovered, and bodies were buried, all save the redcoats - Colonel Richard Glyn

had insisted that the 24th Regiment of Foot would return to bury their own.

Unlike the defeated and depopulated coastal region, Second Division was harassed every step they took along the road to Ulundi. On June 1, Louis Napoléon, the exiled Prince Imperial - a uniformed observer who had made a nuisance of himself from the second he arrived - was killed with a particularly careless scouting party. On June 5, irregular cavalry from Colonel Wood's Flying Column stumbled across some 300 Zulu sheltering in at the base of Ezungeni Mountain.

When they threatened to encircle the irregulars with the Horns of the Buffalo, they beat a fighting retreat. Chelmsford had finally been blessed with some regular cavalry, and the sound of gunfire brought three troop of 17th (The Duke of Cambridge's Own) Lancers dashing forward. With little understanding of Zulu tactics or the broken ground of southern Africa, Lieutenant Colonel Drury Drury-Lowe formed his men up into an extended line and charged. With the Zulu scattered amongst the rocks at the base of the mountain, the Lancers failed to make contact. Driven back by gunfire, the popular young adjutant Lieutenant Frederick Frith was picked off.

Their raison d'etre was to confront tightly packed squares of infantry on the battlefields of Europe and the 17th Lancers limped back to the camp with Frith's body, having discovered their limitations. One observer noted darkly that it was like "chopping wood with a razor."

Despite the laborious advance and the near constant harrying of the Zulu, by mid-June the Second Division had reached the hills overlooking emaKhosini ('the

Place of Kings'). A sacred site, it was the burial place of Cetshwayo's ancestors and where the very earliest Zulu chiefs had ruled. Repeatedly rebuffing attempts by Cetshwayo to negotiate anything short of total capitulation, Chelmsford ordered a Flying Column raid on emaKhosini on June 26. They set light to homesteads that had been there for over a century, and in doing so destroyed the inkatha ye sizwe ya'kwaZulu ('the Coil of the Nation').

Woven from plaited grass in the reign of Shaka the Great, it incorporated strands of inkatha coils from the tribes he conquered and symbolised the unity of the Zulu. Bound up in the plaits were hairs clipped from men slain by Shaka, dirt scraped from the bodies of Zulu Kings in ritual ablutions, and strands of grass dipped in the vomit from mass cleansing ceremonies, all of which imbued it with spiritual significance. A circle nearly two feet across and as thick as a man's leg, the Coil of the Nation was wrapped in snakeskin and commoners were forbidden from even laying eyes on it.

Power Struggle

Sir Garnet Wolseley arrived in Cape Town on the evening June 23 to find that word of his appointment had arrived before him. Sir Henry Bartle Frere and his wife, Catherine, were gracious hosts. Later that evening, the men stayed up talking of the campaign and Frere confided in Wolseley that: "History would show how right he was, and how weak-kneed and cowardly are the present cabinet."

Frere had no room left to manoeuvre so he could afford to be genial. His role in the war was effectively at an end, but Chelmsford was still in the field and determined to claim his victory before ⟫⟫

Wolseley was able to interfere. Chelmsford calculated that he had two weeks - the time it would take his replacement to catch up with him.

By June 28, Second Division were descending the Mthonjaneni Heights, just 17 miles from Ulundi. The Zulu capital was clearly visible beyond the White Mfolozi River when a telegram arrived from Wolseley demanding an immediate situation report: Chelmsford responded that he was fortifying Mthonjaneni and was advancing on Ulundi where he was expecting the Zulu to confront him. He confirmed that the First Division was no longer involved, having fallen so chronically behind in its advance.

The 1864 uniform of the 17th Lancers, as they appeared in the field.

ABOVE · *Lieutenant Colonel Drury Drury-Lowe served with the 17th Lancers in Crimea and the Indian Mutiny.*

On July 1, Wolseley left Durban for Port Durnford on HMS *Shah*, counting on it being quicker than the overland route. He received Chelmsford's report that morning and was now certain the general was about to do something stupid. He issued a final order to halt: "Concentrate your forces immediately, undertake no operations and flash [heliostat] back your moves. Astonished at not hearing from you."

Chelmsford confirmed his receipt of the message but pointedly ignored the orders. Wolseley seethed: "Chelmsford has been pushing on well ahead also since he heard I was likely to be on the spot and supersede him. He has apparently cut himself off from his base to prevent my communicating with him. Nobody knows where he is at the moment, but he and his evil genius, that arch-snob young [John North] Crealock, are now doing all they know to do something brilliant before I can join the troops in the field."

For three days Worseley waited

to land at Port Durnford, but weather just wasn't in his corner. Reluctantly, he ordered the captain to return to Durban and he would join Crealock by riding up the coastal route after all.

RED COATS ON THE WHITE RIVER

Chelmsford was no doubt delighted that his chance of victory had been saved by ill wind and choppy waters. With three laagers entrenched on Mthonjaneni Heights sheltering the non-combatants, the soldiers of Second Division and the Flying Column travelled light. They carried everything they needed with them.

Cetshwayo's emissaries kept coming and Chelmsford kept indulging them. He prevaricated to buy time to cover the dense, thorny bush on the approach to the White Mfolozi. The Royal Engineers led the way,

hacking at the undergrowth with their axes - the wagons and guns following. On the far bank, the rolling plains before Ulundi were the ideal field for tightly packed volleys of Martini-Henry rifles and the charge of the 17th Lancers.

On July 3, with a double laager and Fort Nolela, a redoubt of stone and earthworks, constructed on a knoll overlooking the river, Chelmsford abruptly ended his diplomatic folderol with the Zulu. Second Division were ready to fight.

Cetshwayo may have been desperately hoping for some last-minute reprieve, but his warriors had other ideas and had grown impatient. Across the morning, Zulu snipers had taken shots at the men gathering water in the river and even fired into the double laager.

At midday, the artillery hurled their shells

The Zulu charge the bristling rifles of the British square across open ground.

With the battle won and the shooting war over, Chelmsford sent his victory telegram to the Secretary of State for War, Frederick Stanley, and asked for permission to resign. It was another petulant faux pas, as Wolseley had ordered that all communications go through him. However, Ulundi was his victory and he had earned the right to both celebrate it and to jump before he was pushed.

Wolseley sent a message of sincere congratulations and noted in his journal: "Chelmsford can now return home with a halo of success about him." Almost as soon as their ceasefire had begun, it was ended. Chelmsford packed up most of the Second Division and the Flying Column and returned to Mthonjaneni Heights.

On July 8, a telegram from Chelmsford arrived, having been sent the long way around. In it, he reported that he would take the Flying Column to rendezvous with Wolseley, while the Second Division were being marched back to Fort Newdigate on the Natal border. "A hasty evacuation of the country I now occupy," he wrote, "seems to be advisable at the present moment, and I await your further instructions before carrying it out."

Chelmsford didn't wait. Wolseley was mortified that Ulundi, the capital of the Zulu Kingdom, had simply been abandoned without even a token British presence to project force He ordered Wood's column to remain in the vicinity, but by that point, Chelmsford had already moved them on.

Much later, Buller told his old mentor that the supplies had been perfectly adequate to leave a garrison at Ulundi and he had offered to take 400 men himself and stay. He explained: "It was nervousness and dread of what might come next to diminish the lustre of the crowning victory."

Chelmsford complained to Stanley in an angry, rambling message that he felt humiliated and undermined. Wolseley was surprisingly sympathetic, writing to his wife, Louisa: "He is evidently much put out by being superseded... I feel for him with all my heart, for I know how he must have suffered."

On July 15, Chelmsford arrived with the flying column at Port Durnford. There he met Wolseley. It was civil but awkward, and on July 17 they parted - Wolseley heading for Eshowe, and Chelmsford for Britain.

---

into the bush and Buller's irregular cavalry - a mix of Mounted Infantry, Frontier Light Horse, Baker's Horse, Transvaal Rangers and others - rode out to deal with the snipers. A hundred of them crossed at the main drift in full view, while Buller led another 400 further up the river to cross unseen. Catching the Zulu in a perfect pincer, they bolted, and Buller gave chase - he planned on reconnoitring the way ahead anyhow.

With the irregulars chomping at the bit, Buller was racing towards a 5,000-strong Zulu ambush in the Mbilane Valley when instinct pulled him short. He ordered a halt and the frustrated Zulu broke from cover. Opening fire, they killed three men outright and knocked numerous others from their horses. As the warriors charged, Captain Lord William Beresford, 9th Lancers, dismounted to rescue an NCO who was trapped under his fallen mount.

Catching sight of their plight as they retreated, Buller ordered the Frontier Light Horse to wheel around and push the Zulu back with a volley from their carbines. Sergeant Edmund O'Toole rushed to Beresford's side and they hauled the wounded man into the saddle, just as the Zulu closed around them. With a flash of his sabre, Beresford cut one warrior down and they rode clear.

That night, the men settled down to the eerie chants of the amaButho which had advanced from Ulundi. "With ever increasing shrillness," wrote the war correspondent Charles Fripp, "thousands of exultant voices rose and fell in perfect rhythm, faintly but clearly upon our ears. It was the war chant of thousands of Zulu warriors, whose sonorous voices were bringing songs of devotion to their King through the stillness of the night, swaying their supple bodies and gleaming weapons in fierce unison with their beating feet beneath the same calm moon shining on our silent camp."

THE LITTLE RED MATCHBOX

Rising at 4am the next morning, the army crossed the drift in silence. They left five companies of 1/24th Regiment of Foot - many of them having escaped death at Isandlwana - and the Royal Engineers to hold the double laager and the fort.

The pride of Chelmsford's force was his coveted cavalry, the 17th (The Duke of Cambridge's Own) Lancers - a stirring sight in their blue tunics and gleaming white facing, pennants streaming from their lances - and the 1st King's Dragoon Guards. Used as skirmishers and scouts with swords and carbines, the 1st Dragoons found themselves in action alongside Colonel Buller's volunteer horse.

Chelmsford had six battalions of line infantry, half of them blooded and half of them fresh-faced. 1/13th (1st Somersetshire) (Prince Albert's Light Infantry) Regiment of Foot, 90th Regiment of Foot (Perthshire Volunteers), and 80th Regiment of Foot (Staffordshire Volunteers) had served with Wood at the Battle of Kambula. 2/21st (Royal Scots Fusiliers) Regiment of Foot, 58th (Rutlandshire) Regiment of Foot, and the 94th Regiment of Foot were all newly arrived and yet to stare down the shaft of an iKwla.

On the other side of the river, the army - 4,166 white and 958 black soldiers, 12 artillery pieces and two Gatling guns - formed up into a huge hollow square four ranks deep. The tool carts, water carts, artillery and ammunition wagons trundled safely on the inside of the awkward, slow-moving fortress, while the cavalry patrolled to the sides and ahead. To 16-year old Private 'Lucky' George Mossop of the Frontier Light Horse, it looked like "a little red matchbox about to be trampled to dust by the feet of the Zulu army."

The area around Ulundi was the heart of Zulu power and as the square marched past the military kraal of kwaBulawayo, the rear-guard put it to the torch. On reaching the high ground 700 yards beyond the next garrison, kwaNodwengu, the square came to a halt. It was roughly 8am. The artillery and the Gatling guns took their place on the sides, facing outwards and the men turned too.

Already the Zulu were beginning to circle, and some 15,000 to 20,000 warriors were ready to fight, but the King they fought for was long gone. Cetshwayo had fled with his family to a distant kraal, while his generals and advisors watched the final act of a free Zulu Kingdom from a remote hill.

The mounted screen goaded the Zulu, drawing them into range before retreating towards the square. The redcoats parted like the Dead Sea in finely drilled formation to allow the cavalry safely inside. "We set fire to one of their kraals," recalled Private George Turnham, 17th Lancers, "and this seemed to be the signal for the beginning of the fight. No sooner did the Zulus see smoke then they came running out of their hiding places like a swarm of bees."

Just before 9am, cannon opened fire followed by the rattle of the Gatling guns and finally, the thunder crack of hundreds of rifles firing in volley, the first two ranks kneeling and the second standing. Each rank fired one after another in a continuous ripple, pausing only for the smoke to clear. "[The Zulu] were falling down in heaps, as though they had been tipped out of carts," said Corporal William Roe, 58th Regiment.

Though the newcomers were awed by their first glimpse of the Zulu in battle, the old hands could see none of the fighting spirit that had brought them so close to death before. The veteran amaButho - the inGobamakhosi, iNdluyengwe, uThulwana and uVe - mustered their last reserves of energy for a final attempt to crack open the square. They crept into a patch of dead ground and suddenly launched themselves at the right corner from 130 yards.

Captain Guy Dawnay, Natal Native Contingent, recalled: "Our fire didn't check them the least; nearer they came - 100 yards - 80 yards - still rushing on, a thick black mass. Lord Chelmsford came galloping up, telling the 58th and 21st to fire faster; Newdigate pulled out his revolver. The 9-pounder crashed through them again and again; but at that short distance the canister did not burst."

"It was a fearful sight," said Roe. "You could not see many yards in front for the dense cloud of smoke from our guns. We made up our mind to fight in close quarter with our bayonets, and swords, but the enemy began to shake in front of our fire, and halted dead for a few seconds, then turned around and flew for their lives."

THE WORLD AFLAME

Within 30 minutes the attacks were over, and the cavalry were ordered out of the square to put the enemy to flight. Finally unleashed, the 17th Lancers ran down an estimated 150 Zulu over three miles. Dawnay joined them, writing gleefully: "The first man I reached turned around with shield in left hand and assegais and gun in right. [My sword] cut clean half-way down the shield, hit something hard, caught the Zulu on the neck I think; down he went, and the next minute a lance went through him."

In a letter his mother shared with the press, one dragoon recalled: "We galloped as hard as we could, but the Zulus ran very nearly as fast as we, so instead of losing time in dismounting we, with one consent halted and fired."

Once the Zulu reached the hills and made a final attempt to regroup, the cavalry retreated, and guns were wheeled forwards. "Oh! How they bolted," cheered Mr France, a civilian wagon master. "But to little purpose, for shell after shell followed them and told most effectively on them." The 17th Lancers counted 150

A 17th Lancer and 1st Dragoon riding side-by-side, both wearing dress uniforms. The Lancer's four-pointed helmet is a Polish design called a czapka.

dead, returning with their lances red with gore, and the irregulars, Mounted Infantry, and 1st Dragoons claimed another 450. The total Zulu dead for the battle, which lasted under an hour, was around 1,500. It was the largest toll inflicted on the Zulu in a single exchange of the entire war.

On the British side, three officers and 10 other ranks were dead and around 70 wounded. Chelmsford ordered the column to the bank of the Mbilane stream to rest and take food, while the cavalry was sent to burn Ulundi. The actual honour of setting the royal kraal alight would go to the Frontier Light Horse as chief among the irregulars, but there was mad dash among the more aristocratic of the cavalry who all fancied being able to claim that they had been the first into Ulundi.

Beresford won the race, causing one of Chelmsford's intelligence officers, the (by some accounts, drunk) Honourable William Drummond, to storm off in a

huff. The third son of a viscount turned colonial adventurer, Drummond had been in Zululand for years and his greatest claim to fame was shooting 23 hippos in a single morning. That day he might have understood how the hippos had felt as he blundered into a group of Zulu stragglers and was butchered.

Watching from the distance, Roe recalled, "In a very short time, the whole of the King's city, Ulundi, was in flames. This was a fearful sight to see. You would think the whole world was on fire when there was a dense mass of flames seven miles in length."

As the ebullient men marched back to the double laager on the White Umfolozi River, the band striking up *Rule Britannia* and *God Save the Queen*, "We passed several dead Zulus, all of whom having their stomachs ripped open; this was done by our natives, who, as soon as the battle was over, began to get plucky and went about killing the wounded without mercy."

The 17th Lancers form up and trade stories while the Zulu capital burns.

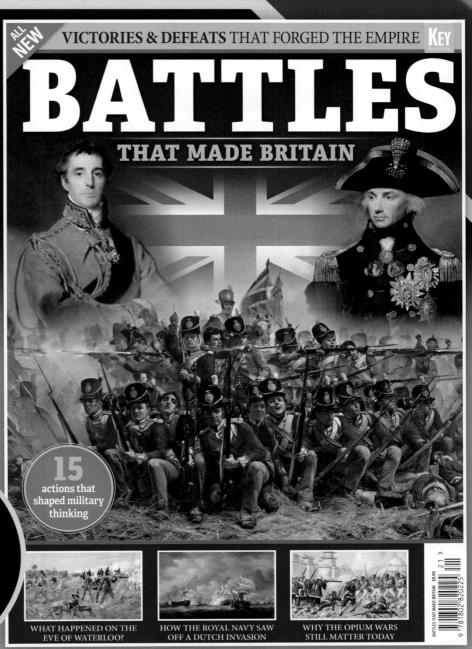

SEDUCED by GLORY

The Death of the Prince Imperial

One of history's strangest, yet most tragic ironies is that the last male-line heir to Napoléon Bonaparte, Emperor of France, died fighting for Britain.

Louis Napoléon, Prince Imperial was the grandson of Napoléon's brother, Louis Bonaparte, by the infamous Emperor's stepdaughter, Hortense de Beauharnais. His own father Emperor Napoléon III, humiliated by defeat in the Franco-Prussian War, was tossed from the throne in 1870. He found refuge in England with his wife, Eugénie de Montijo, and his son.

They ended up in a country house in Chislehurst, Kent where he passed away in 1873, ruminating on the French defeat at the Battle of Sedan. Regarded as upstarts by most of Europe's ruling dynasties, Queen Victoria found Napoléon III charming and took a keen interest in his successor

ENGLAND'S EMPEROR

Even before his father's exile, the Prince Imperial was an Anglophile. His British nurse, Miss Shaw, had been recommended by Queen Victoria and she taught him English from an early age. He had seen conflict first hand too, when war broke out he was only 14 years old and he accompanied his father to the frontlines at Saarbrücken where the imperial party came under fire from the Prussians. Louis relished the sight and sounds of the cannon booming, the walking wounded limping back from the front, and the gallant French army in charging towards the foe.

He studied physics at King's College London - another minor irony, it was founded by Arthur Wellesley, 1st Duke of Wellington who had defeated his great-uncle at the Battle of Waterloo - albeit it as

a poor student. Rather than complete his studies there, Louis was admitted to the Royal Military Academy, Woolwich, the finishing school for officers of the Royal Artillery and Royal Engineers. Artillery being, of course, the family business.

The Prince Imperial was a serious-minded young man, with a level of pomposity that fit his station. He complained of his fellow students at King's incessantly whistling and responded to the joshing of his fellow officer cadets with "Is it an insult?" which provoked even greater mirth, but as his English improved he came into his own.

The governor of the Royal Military Academy, Sir Lintorn Simmons, reported that the prestigious cadet was a model student and "by his invariable punctuality and exactitude in the performance of his duties, by his perfect respect for authority

Mort du Prince Impérial by Paul Jamin. With his death, he was elevated to national hero and an intense period of Anglophobia followed, with some even claiming his death was a conspiracy by Queen Victoria.

The Prince Imperial wearing a cavalry-style Royal Artillery mess jacket with vest, which despite decades of military reform was largely unchanged from the Napoleonic Wars. The 'Austrian knot' on the sleeve identifies this as a lieutenant's jacket. Note the lack of regimental insignia on his collar, a reminder that the Prince was unable to hold a commission in the British Army.

and submission to discipline, has set an example which deserves honourable mention among his comrades."

Louis graduated from Woolwich seventh out of his class of 34, and first in horsemanship and fencing. One of the War Office's conditions of him being allowed to study at Woolwich was that he would not be able to join the British Army. As one of the top ten graduates, he would have been automatically entitled to a commission in the Royal Engineers, but his keen sense of legacy drove him to announce that if he had the option he would have joined the Royal Artillery instead.

By the outbreak of the Anglo-Zulu War in 1879, the Prince Imperial had proved his panache in manoeuvres with an artillery battery and had been romantically linked to Princess Beatrice, the youngest daughter of Queen Victoria and Prince Albert. In weird synchronicity, Beatrice would eventually marry another problematic foreign prince with a desire to serve - Prince Henry of Battenberg - and like the Prince Imperial he would die serving in one of Britain's African campaigns, in his case the Gold Coast.

When the reserves were mustered in the aftermath of the Battle of Isandlwana, the 23-year-old Prince Imperial begged for permission to go with them. Campaigning

ABOVE · *The last photograph taken of Napoléon III following his exile to Great Britain.*

LEFT · *A view of the Prince Imperial statue, gazing on his old alma mater. In this postcard, you can clearly see the polished granite plinth flanked by four bronze eagles.*

was his calling, but also burnishing his laurels in battle would prove him a worthy Emperor-in-waiting.

The Prime Minister, Benjamin Disraeli, objected strongly on the basis that the French government would find it provocative, but the Prince's mother - stung by her son's distress - pressured Prince George, Duke of Cambridge and Queen Victoria. Cambridge, Commander-in-Chief and cousin of the Queen, hit upon the idea of attaching the Prince Imperial to Chelmsford's staff as a 'civilian observer'. An exasperated Disraeli wrote to a

ABOVE · *The Prince Imperial pictured in Natal, he wears the braided patrol jacket of a Royal Artillery lieutenant.*

ABOVE · *Dowager Empress Eugénie was escorted to the site of her son's death by Colonel Wood in 1880, where she planted this stone cross on behalf of Queen Victoria.*

ABOVE · *The discovery of the Prince Imperial's remains. Immensely popular with his peers (if not the men entrusted with his care), his death shocked the entire army.*

colleague: "I am quite mystified by that little abortion, the Prince Imperial."

PRINCE IMPETUOUS

Explaining that he was to take charge of Louis, Cambridge had warned the general: "My only anxiety on his conduct would be, that he is too plucky and go ahead."

The Prince Imperial relished army life and his urge to show off remained undimmed by years among the more standoffish Anglais: he could vault into the saddle from a run, and at a gallop would slice thrown potatoes with the sword that his great-uncle had carried at the Battle of Austerlitz (1805).

Chelmsford thought he'd stumbled across the perfect billet for the Prince Imperial, something that would get him away from danger but satisfy his hunger for adventure. Colonel Richard Harrison, Royal Engineers had been recently appointed Acting Quartermaster General responsible for surveying Zululand ahead of Brevet Colonel Evelyn Wood's Flying Column, sketching maps of the area they traversed and filling in details of enemy forces.

Louis took to the role with enthusiasm but seizing on an opportunity to see Zululand for himself, he joined a patrol of Frontier Light Horse. Convincing Harrison he would be perfectly safe with an escort that strong, he quickly displayed the 'pluck' that the Duke of Cambridge feared, shooting off ahead of the troop with his sword drawn in pursuit of some Zulu scouts. Liuetenant Colonel Redvers Buller, commanding the Frontier Light Horse, was furious.

He told Harrison he would not accept responsibility for the Prince Imperial again.

After some pleading from Louis, Harrison next fobbed him off onto a troop of Natal Horse. It was with these colonial rough riders that the dashing Prince Imperial with neatly pressed Royal Artillery undress uniform got his chance to draw blood when chancing upon a small occupied kraal on a rocky kopje. Skirmishing with its inhabitants and driving them off, they found the huts filled with loot from Isandlwana.

By the time the patrol returned, Buller had made a formal complaint to Chelmsford for the Prince's impetuous

behaviour. The general ordered that he should be confined to camp and reduced to sketching its immediate locale unless Harrison could guarantee a decent sized escort for his safety.

AMBUSH IN ZULULAND

By now, it was becoming abundantly clear that the haughty heir would get his way, and he was allowed out on a scouting mission on June 1, 1879 to an area Harrison believed free of the Zulu.

Accompanied by seven mounted troopers and under the command of Lieutenant Jahleel Brenton Carey, who as a French-speaking Guernseyman was thought

ABOVE · *The site of the Prince Imperial's death, photographed shortly afterwards and marked by a simple stone cairn.*

could act a thunderous volley tore into the kraal. The horses began to panic as the men desperately mounted and 40 Zulu warriors charged out of the long grass bellowing their war cries. The Prince Imperial was caught with only one foot in the stirrup and he flung himself over the saddle. Another Guernseyman, a trooper called Le Tocq, called out "Dépêchez-vous, s'il vous plait, Votre Altesse!" ('Hurry up, please, Your Highness!") as he galloped past.

His stirrup snapped from taking the Prince's entire weight and the last they saw was Louis slip from his saddle and under the hooves of his bolting mount.

His arm broken, and his sword lost, the Prince Imperial drew his revolver and tried to run but was soon surrounded by the nimble Zulu. Seven of them had the prince cornered and an assegai sailed through the air and into his thigh, he pulled it out and rushed at his attacker, who stepped deftly aside. Another assegai struck the Prince in his left shoulder, he batted aside their spears for a few seconds before blood loss dropped him to a sitting position.

By the time the patrol had regained control of their startled horses, it was too late. The heir to the French throne had been finished off by a flurry of blades.

Four of the party were missing, including the Prince, and as Carey limped back to camp he knew with that his career in the British Army was over. Meeting a mounted patrol led by Buller, the battle-hardened cavalry commander snarled at the broken youth: "You ought to be shot, and I hope you will be."

END OF THE ADVENTURE

The next morning a force of nearly a thousand rode out to recover the body of the Prince Imperial and his three comrades.

His body had been stripped naked save a gold chain with a medal of the Virgin Mary and the seal of his great uncle and dumped in the donga. Seventeen wounds were counted, and his life ended with an assegai into his heart and another through his right eye for good measure. He had fought to the end, his arms were latticed with defensive wounds and tangled into a cold fist was a clump of black hair.

Wrapped in a Tricolore and carried on a gun carriage, a Roman Catholic funeral was held for the Prince Imperial at the camp with Chelmsford marching numbly behind the body. He was embalmed by the battlefield surgeons as best they could and carried back to Durban by horse-drawn ambulance.

Empress Eugénie spent two days lost in her grief, neither eating or speaking. Within a decade she had lost her husband, her son, and all hope of returning to France in imperial glory. There was more horror to come, when the coffin was prised open they discovered the battlefield embalming was so botched that the Prince Imperial's face was unrecognisable and he could only be identified by his teeth and a childhood scar.

When his possessions were returned to Chislehurst, the Dowager Empress was confronted with his bloodied, tattered uniform recovered from the donga, and the broken saddle that had sealed her son's fate. She fainted on the spot.

Noble in her grief, Eugénie channelled her energy into a monument to her lost family, founding the Benedictine abbey of St Michael's in Farnborough as an imperial crypt for two generations of Bonaparte, moving both Louis Napoléon and Napoléon III from their graves at St Mary's, Chislehurst. ◀◀◀

capable of appealing to the Prince's fraternal instincts, they were instructed to wait for reinforcements from the Natal Native Horse to form a more substantial patrol. Carey and Louis were as rash as each other, and the former found himself deferring to the latter, who grew impatient and decided to set off without their support

After a day of riding and sketching the landscape, they settled in a deserted kraal surrounded by long grass and ominously close to a deep donga. They got some coffee brewing and the two young men began an animated discussion about the military career of Napoléon Bonaparte. No pickets were posted, and even when their guide pointed out the still warm ashes in front of one of the huts, the two young men brushed it off.

Half an hour later, the guide spotted a single Zulu on a nearby rise but before they

BELOW · *Natal police line the streets of Durban and flags fly at half-mast as the Prince Imperial's body arrives.*

THE KING OVER THE WATER

The Capture of Cetshwayo and the Fall of the Zulu

Lieutenant General Frederic Thesiger, Lord Chelmsford sailed from Natal on July 27, 1879, somehow feeling as though he had both lost and won the war. He was not the same man he had been two years earlier, the guilt and insecurity that had plagued him since Isandlwana had never left and brushing up against Wolseley was a reminder of just how low his stock had sunk back in Britain.

He never saw active service again but went instead to fight for his reputation in the press and the House of Lords. He never lost the faith of Queen Victoria, though. She appointed him as a Knight Grand Cross of the Order of the Bath (GCB) on August 19, 1879. On his retirement, she bestowed on him the title of Lieutenant of the Tower of London and by the time he died in 1905 at the age of 78, having suffered a seizure in the middle of a billiards match in the United Service Club, he had accumulated numerous courtesy titles and posts.

His culpability for the early disasters of the Anglo-Zulu War still divides historians as fiercely as they divided public opinion of his day. Roughly 1,430 white soldiers lost their lives in the conflict, and over a thousand black auxiliaries. The numbers of Africans slain on the British side is impossible to calculate because too little interest was shown in accounting for them while they lived.

A FOND FAREWELL

Wars don't end on the battlefield and Sir Garnet Wolseley set to work. After dressing down the flamboyant Major General Henry Hope Crealock whose First Division had spent the Battle of Ulundi pottering uselessly around the Zulu coast ("[They] might as well have been marching along the Woking and Aldershot road," he wrote in his journal), he brought in some of his trusted commanders to see through the final stages of the war, but he had two old favourites to say farewell to first.

Brevet Colonel Evelyn Wood and

BRITISH BENEVOLENCE.
"It is painful to be obliged to use force against the weak."—*Earl Granville in House of Lords.*

**ABOVE · ** *An 1882 cover of the satirical magazine Puck shows Britain having defeated the Zulu, Boers, Afghan, Ashanti, and Egyptians. Were it all that easy...*

Lieutenant Colonel Redvers Buller were both going home. Wolseley tried to entice them to stay, but they were running on empty. Wood hadn't had a full night's sleep in eight months and was on the cusp of a nervous breakdown, while Buller's legs were riddled with open, oozing sores from his endless hours in the saddle.

LEFT · *The defeated Zulu chiefs sign up to Sir Garnet Wolseley's new constitution for the division of Zululand.*

BELOW · *Major Marter and the 1st Dragoons take the surrender of Cetshwayo.*

The night before they were presented to Wolseley, Wood had ordered the Flying Column scrub the dirty improvised camouflage from their sun helmets and their valise webbing. Their tunics were tattered, and their boots scuffed, their skin scabbed and sunburnt, but the whites gleamed proudly.

As Wood and Buller departed, the men of the 90th Regiment of Foot (Perthshire Volunteers) (Light Infantry) and 1st/13th (1st Somersetshire) (Prince Albert's Light Infantry) Regiment of Foot cried out, "Godspeed you!" bringing the weary Wood to the verge of tears: "We had served together, one battalion eight months, and the other for 18 months. Much of the time had been fraught with anxiety; the goodbye of these men, of whom it is commonly said in South Africa, 'I worked their souls out', and of whom I had treated with the sternest discipline, was such that I have never forgotten."

A more unlikely scene in the Anglo-Zulu War it's impossible to imagine, but the bullish Buller went one further and burst into tears at leaving his beloved Frontier Light Horse behind. They had been together for over two years, through the 9th Frontier War (1877-1878) and the 1st Anglo-BaPedi War (1878), and of course the long hard fight through northern Zululand, moulding a highly professional, capable and courageous body held in uniquely high regard for colonials.

"Wherever the stiffest place was he was sure to be found," recalled Commandant Frank Streatfield, who led Mfengu levies in the 9th Frontier War. "In action if you ascertain for certain where the most bullets were flying, you could be pretty safe in venturing your last dollar that Buller would be in the middle of it."

THE VICTOR'S JUSTICE

Chelmsford's withdrawal from Zululand in the wake of his victory at Ulundi had left Wolseley with a substantial mess to clean up. The absence of a British force in northern Zululand had given King Cetshwayo kaMpande heart and he had already gathered fresh warriors around him, recruited from the Mandlakazi clan (founded by a cousin of Shaka the Great).

Wolseley's vision for Zululand was to see the nation broken up into new districts, with the 'white iNduna' John Dunn - who he thought was untrustworthy but useful - the most powerful chief, responsible for the region directly abutting Natal. This plan would be threatened by having the Zulu King at large and those chiefs who had defected would return to Cetshwayo once the British had pulled back entirely.

"I feel there is nothing for it," he recorded, "but to return with a force to Ulundi ⟫⟫⟫

THE LAST KING OF THE ZULU

ABOVE · *The 15-year old Dinuzulu kaCetshwayo in 1883, wearing traditional dress.*

ABOVE · *Dinuzulu in 1907, by which time he had inherited his father's powerful build.*

Aged only 16, Dinuzulu kaCetshwayo was proclaimed King of the Zulu on May 20, 1884 by Cetshwayo's remaining iNdunas.

With the uSuthu crippled by the attack on Ulundi, they sought allies in the Transvaal to wage war on the man he blamed for his father's death, Zibhebhu kaMaphitha. They obliged him with a company of 350 Boers, commanded by Lucas Meyer and including a young Louis Botha, who would be a thorn in the side of Britain during both Boer Wars. In return, Dinuzulu ceded a 5,300-square-mile stretch of Zululand to the Afrikaners, which became the short-lived Nieuwe Republiek.

Dinuzulu's 2,000 uSuthu and the 350 mounted Boers set out from the Transvaal Republic and marched into Zululand, where the Boers proclaimed him King and anointed him with a bottle of castor oil. With only 3,000 Mandlakazi to fight

the boy King's growing uSuthu army and his fair-weather friends, Zibhebhu's men were slaughtered. The usurper escaped and was granted refuge by the British, while Dinuzulu ruled as a puppet King of his Boer neighbours, who began extending their own borders rapaciously.

The expansion of the Nieuwe Republiek was of concern to Britain where the collapse of the Zulu state wasn't. Britain moved to reassert its authority over Zululand, the Nieuwe Republiek's borders were fixed, and although Natal still wasn't granted the authority to annex Zululand, the Natal Native Law Code was extended to the Zulu and enforced by the Natal Mounted Police. Zululand was declared a British protectorate and its King was treated the same as any other chief.

Dinuzulu insisted on enforcing Zulu laws without British approval, he maintained a standing army, refused to pay tax, and imported rifles from the Boers. Dinuzulu was

hauled before the Natal governor, Lord Arthur Havelock, who snarled: "The rule of the House of Shaka is a thing of the past. It is dead. It is like water split on the ground. The Queen now rules in Zululand and no one else."

If Dinuzulu was approaching tipping point, the return of Zibhebhu pushed him over the edge. His old enemy had been permitted to return and the lands the Mandlakazi claimed were now occupied by the uSuthu. The outcome was inevitable and so were the consequences. Though Dinuzulu emerged victorious over Zibhebhu a second time, British tolerance had been exhausted.

The young King was arrested, convicted of treason and exiled to the South Atlantic island of St Helena, which had once caged Napoléon Bonaparte. Taking his uncles and his wives, he learnt to write and compose music on the piano and organ, converted to Christianity, and started a family on the island before he could return home with the status of an 'ordinary' chief in 1897.

Overestimating his appeal as a figurehead, Dinuzulu was accused of treason and sedition for an imagined role in the Bambatha Rebellion of 1906. In 1908 the sentence was passed and Dinuzulu was imprisoned a second time. Fortunately, he was released only two years into this second sentence when his old friend Louis Botha became the first Prime Minister of the Union of South Africa. The last King of the Zulu to be recognised as such, Dinuzulu kaCetshwayo died aged 45 in the highlands of Transvaal on October 18, 1913.

He summed up his own life in 1907, saying: "My sole crime is that I am a son of Cetshwayo. My trouble is like that of no one else. It beset me when I was a child and my father was taken by the white people, and it is still besetting me. I could not bury Cetshwayo, my father; he died while I was being chased... what is grievous is to be killed and yet alive. To die outright is nothing, for one rests and does not feel trouble."

and dictate terms to everyone from thence. Cetshwayo must either be killed or taken prisoner or driven from Zululand before this war is considered over."

Wolseley summoned the coastal tribes, many of whom had already surrendered to Crealock, and outlined his new plan. He assured them that Zululand would

remain the home of the Zulu and although the Kingdom of the Zulu was over, its chiefs would remain autonomous. He would announce the new paramount chiefs of each district at Ulundi in a few days' time.

The coastal Zulu were encouraged, but the northern chiefs were less easily cowed, most of them had only vestigial ties to their

monarch and were doubly resistant to any new authority. Still, Wolseley asked them to meet him at Ulundi on August 10.

As he embarked for the ruined capital, he was presented with a grovelling message from Cetshwayo, who was deeply sorry for any transgression and just wanted to be left alone. A second message followed later

Vjin had been promised plenty of cattle if he persuaded Wolseley to leave him his kingdom, but he accepted a counter offer of £200 for leading a troop of British cavalry to Cetshwayo's hideout. Unfortunately, by the time they arrived there, the fugitive monarch had already moved on.

REGIME CHANGE

Perhaps swung by the unedifying sight of their King scampering from kraal to kraal, on August 14, five of the most prominent northern chiefs presented themselves to Wolseley, along with 150 lesser chiefs and a tribute of royal cattle. Those now looking to negotiate their futures including Mnyamana kaNgqengelele, Cetshwayo's chief minister, and Tshingwayo kaMahole, who had led the Zulu at Isandlwana. On August 16, the King's favourite brother, Ziwedu kaMpande, joined them, and later in the month, others turned themselves in.

ABOVE · *The King, his wives and his retinue board a surfboat at Port Durnford. The escort repeatedly noted his grace and he made a point to bid them farewell.*

BELOW · *His thighs too thick to ride a horse and finding that the jolting of a cart made him queasy, Cetshwayo chose to walk to Wolseley's camp at Ulundi.*

LEFT · *Captain Lord Gifford was mentioned in dispatches for his role in finding Cetshwayo. He blindfolded two Zulu children at a kraal he believed the King had taken refuge in and staged a mock execution until one confessed.*

asking that the King be granted a kraal where he could live as a private citizen, bothering no-one. Wolseley replied that if he surrendered, he would be treated well, but privately hoped "some amiable assassin would kill him."

The only man waiting for Wolseley at Ulundi was Cornelius Vjin. A Dutch trader who found himself on the wrong side of the border when the war broke out, he had spent the last few months with Cetshwayo's court and he presented the latest terms. The King knew full well that a deposed chief wouldn't survive long in Zulu society, so Vjin asked that Cetshwayo retain his title.

Wolseley wasn't massively interested in their cattle. He wanted their guns and he held the men hostage until their retainers scurried back to their kraals to gather up their muskets, spears, and the Martini-Henrys looted from the dead of Isandlwana. However, Cetshwayo himself remained at large and a small circle of northern tribes continued to protect him, including Wood's old nemeses from the disastrous Battle of Hlobane, the abaQulusi.

Wolseley began to apply pressure on Mnyamana, who eventually gave his King up. He revealed that he was hiding out in a kraal belonging to one of Mnyamana's subordinate chiefs, Mkhosana. There, the King and his host were shielded from the British scouts and John Dunn's vast tribal intelligence network by the deep Ngome Forest. Two British patrols were

ABOVE · *A striking portrait of Cetshwayo taken on his visit to London, his carefully cultivated nobility is obvious.*

RIGHT · *An editorial cartoon from the King's visit shows him presenting an endless parade of wives. In fact, his party travelled without women to avoid reminding the British that he was polygamous.*

dispatched to bring the King in; one under Captain Edric Frederick Gifford, 3rd Baron Gifford, Wolseley's aide-de-camp, and another under Major Richard Marter, 1st King's Dragoon Guards.

Cetshwayo had been on the run for two months, but he couldn't outrun Gifford. The captain had earned his Victoria Cross commanding Wolseley's jungle scouts during the 3rd Anglo-Ashanti War (1873-1874), and his patrol lived off the land, looting kraals for provisions, torturing captured Zulu for information, and following tracks through the forest. On August 28, he found the kraal.

Advancing stealthily, Gifford deployed his men on the approaches to the village and waited for dusk to pounce. However, he was beaten to the prize by Marter, whose party had approached from the opposite direction and found themselves looking down on the kraal from a ridge, some 2,000 feet up.

Removing their scabbards and anything else that might rattle and give them away, Marter's 1st Dragoons descended the ridge in silence, taking the kraal by surprise (and Gifford too, when he found out). "The King was a long time before he would surrender to us," recalled Sergeant R Smith,

1st Dragoons, "but he was told that if he did not come out, we should burn him out, so he quietly came out, and looked as stately as a general coming to review a few thousand men on parade."

NEW RULERS AND NEW WARS

Cetshwayo held himself aloof as he walked into the camp with his servants and wives, his composure dropping only once as the blackened ruin of Ulundi came into view. "He stopped," wrote Marter, "and placing his hands upon the top of his long staff, rested his forehead upon them for about a minute - then, raising his head,

Cetshwayo in European clothes walks on the wall of the Cape Town bastion in which he was imprisoned, 1882.

he threw off all signs of depression, and marched onwards and into the camp with the most perfect dignity."

Marter led the King through a corridor of soldiers, bayonets fixed, and into Wolseley's tent. There, the general told him that he was formally deposed for having broken the bogus coronation oaths, his land would be sundered, and he would be imprisoned. Within four hours he was on his way to Port Durnford and the ocean liner SS *Natal*, where the first-time sailor was violently seasick.

As the King departed for Cape Town under armed escort, the Zulu holdouts surrendered. Wolseley divided Zululand into 13 districts, with those on the borders given to chiefs who had fought alongside the British, already had autonomy from Cetshwayo, or had surrendered early enough to earn the distrust of their fellows, while those in the interior were minor leaders with little influence. The unpopular border chiefs would depend on the British to cling to power, while the interior chiefs would be too low status to rally any serious support for a rebellion or their own claims to the throne.

A British Resident was established in Eshowe, effectively a colonial viceroy who would replace the Zulu King as the region's central power, but there was no means of backing up his empty title. Zululand hadn't been annexed, despite Natal's white settlers hungrily eying up the vast tracts of fertile land. What Zululand became was little more than a failed state masquerading as a client state. Wolseley's carefully crafted lack of unity would inspire its own problems as civil war broke out. In short, divide and rule had too much division and not enough ruling.

Around 8,000 Zulu had been slain and many more injured, their most important resource - cattle - had been stolen in their thousands, their crops had been left to rot in the fields, and their kraals lay in ruins.

The withdrawal of the last British troops in September 1879 opened space for new conflicts to grow. Resentment to British rule finally ignited on December 20, 1880 and the Transvaal Boers fought and won their independence. It was a humiliating defeat for the little-loved idea of confederation in southern Africa and made the terrible death and destruction of the Anglo-Zulu War politically meaningless.

The King in Exile

In a curious postscript to the affair, following his imprisonment in Cape Town, Cetshwayo kaMpande emerged as a figure of fascination to the British press. He constantly agitated for a return to the throne to restore order over the anarchy and infighting. This spooked the white settlers who had moved into Zululand and Natal Colony who were fearful of a resurgent Zulu Kingdom out for revenge.

In August 1882, Cetshwayo was given permission to visit London and present his case in person. It was as much a carefully scripted public relationships exercise (he took no women with him, as his polygamy would have been received poorly) as it was a genuine attempt to twist the arm of the British government. His regal bearing and perfect composure won him admirers across the empire. Reporters praised his neat European clothes, as though all expectations had been turned on their head the minute he had gotten dressed that morning

A reporter for the *Illustrated London News* gushed: "In his demeanour Cetshwayo is most gentle, utterly belying the popular conception which pictures him as a rude and turbulent savage." Cetshwayo toured major cities, speaking to reporters and parliamentarians alike and, for lack of a better word, schmoozing. Wherever he went he was followed by debate about the injustice of the war and the consequences of his overthrow, but racist caricatures followed too, and many saw the King as a 'rude and turbulent savage' playing dress-up.

The publicity circus rendered lawmakers in Natal incandescent. "I hope the world will know that none of us wish these chiefs back again," bellowed the politician J C Boshoff in the colony's council chamber. "Let them have a pension if you like; let them sit at big dinners in London, but never let them come back to Natal again."

In the end, Cetshwayo's cause won out. The Liberal government of William Gladstone was generally opposed to the gung-ho colonialism of the previous administration, and the King was given back a third of his lands, with another third acting as a buffer state to appease the hysterical Natal. Unfortunately, once shattered, the Zulu Kingdom could not be repaired. Zibhebhu kaMaphitha of the Mandlakazi - one of the 13 'kinglets' appointed by Wolseley - had spent the previous few years nurturing his regal ambitions and Cetshwayo's restoration had put plenty of noses out of joint.

Assembling a coalition of aggrieved chiefs under Zibhebhu's leadership was

ABOVE · *Zibhebhu kaMaphitha photographed in 1880. With Cetshwayo imprisoned, the capable warlord began to consolidate power for himself.*

CETSHWAYO c.1832-1884 King of the Zulus stayed here in 1882

LEFT · *An English Heritage plaque on 18 Melbury Road, London commemorates the King's residence during his visit.* SPUDGUN67 CC BY-SA 4.0

easy enough and on July 22, 1883 Zibhebhu attacked Cetshwayo's new kraal at Ulundi, accompanied by Boer mercenaries. With hundreds of his loyal uSuthu faction slain, the wounded King sought refuge with the British Resident at Eshowe, where he died on February 8, 1884. Some said he had been poisoned, others say he died of a broken heart, which is closer to the truth - it was a heart attack.

Cetshwayo's son, Dinuzulu kaCetshwayo, then took up the uSuthu cause and with Boer support defeated Zibhebhu and was proclaimed King of the now reduced Zulu Kingdom. The Zulu were a broken people, disillusioned with their chiefs, who had either bowed to the British or to the Boers,

Finally, in 1887, Britain could prolong the inevitable no longer. They had broken it, so they had to buy it. The Colony of Zululand was created, a decade later it was incorporated into the Colony of Natal. Then in 1910, three decades after the dangerous dream of federation had blossomed in the reckless minds of Sir Theophilus Shepstone, Sir Henry Bartle Frere and Frederic Thesiger, Lord Chelmsford, Natal joined the Union of South Africa.

THE BRAVEST DEED I EVER SAW

Victoria Cross Heroes of the Anglo-Zulu War

CORPORAL WILLIAM WILSON ALLEN
2/24TH REGIMENT OF FOOT
JANUARY 22-23, 1879
BATTLE OF RORKE'S DRIFT,
NATAL COLONY

Enlisting in York at the age of 15, Allen (or Allan) was a typical Tommy who was dealt his fair share of body blows but kept his chin up. He had been demoted from sergeant because of his alcoholism but married in 1876 and started a family at Brecon where the regiment had been recently relocated. Three years later, the 34-year-old found himself giving covering fire at Rorke's Drift. Despite being shot in the left shoulder he held the besieging Zulu back from the field hospital, keeping lines of communication clear, and gave patients a chance to escape.

RIGHT · *William Wilson Allen wearing a glengarry cap and cap badge while a sergeant instructor in musketry, suggesting the photograph was taken after the Childers Reforms of 1881 but before the glengarry was phased out around the turn of the century.*

RIGHT · *A round-up of the Anglo-Zulu War Victoria Cross winners from the Penny Illustrated Paper showing, clockwise from the top left, Surgeon James Henry Reynolds, Private Samuel Wassall, Lieutenant Browne, Lieutenant Colonel Redvers Buller, and Major William Knox-Leet.*

Even when his arm finally gave way, Allen's wounds were dressed, and he returned to the firing line to keep his comrades supplied with ammunition well into the night. His Victoria Cross was awarded by Her Majesty on December 9, 1879 and although he never regained full use of his left arm, Allen did regain his stripes. He was appointed sergeant instructor in musketry at 3rd Militia Battalion in Brecon and the 4th Volunteer Battalion in Monmouth.

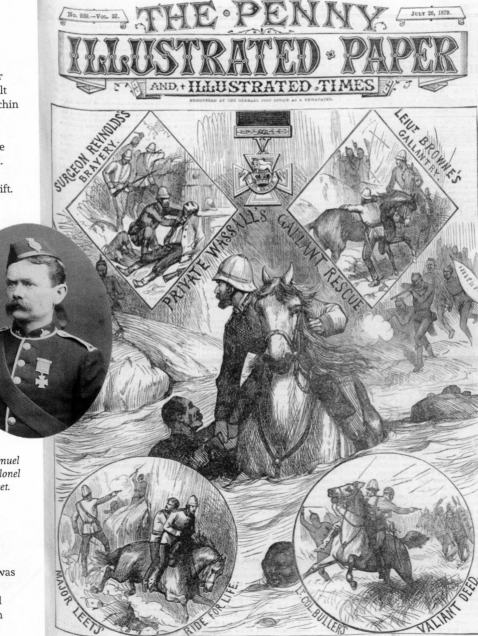

No. 939.—Vol. 37. JULY 26, 1879.

THE PENNY ILLUSTRATED PAPER

AND ILLUSTRATED TIMES

REGISTERED AT THE GENERAL POST OFFICE AS A NEWSPAPER.

SURGEON REYNOLDS'S BRAVERY.

LIEUT BROWNE'S GALLANTRY.

PRIVATE WASSALL'S GALLANT RESCUE.

MAJOR LEET'S RIDE FOR LIFE.

LT.-COL BULLER'S VALIANT DEED.

DEEDS OF BRITISH VALOUR WHICH WON THE VICTORIA CROSS IN ZULULAND.

THE ILLUSTRATED LONDON NEWS,

REGISTERED AT THE GENERAL POST-OFFICE FOR TRANSMISSION ABROAD.

No. 2099.—Vol. LXXV.   SATURDAY, SEPTEMBER 6, 1879.   WITH WHOLE SHEET SUPPLEMENT   SIXPENCE. By Post, 6½d.

LORD WILLIAM BERESFORD'S ENCOUNTER WITH A ZULU IN THE RECONNAISSANCE ACROSS THE UMVOLOSI, JULY 3.—SEE PAGE 218.
FROM A SKETCH BY OUR SPECIAL ARTIST.

Allen passed away in 1890 aged around 46 following an outbreak of Influenza. A fund was quickly raised to provide for his large family. He is buried at Monmouth Cemetery (although his headstone spells his surname "Allan") and his medals are held by the Regimental Museum of the Royal Welsh in Brecon.

Captain Lord William Leslie de la Poer Beresford
9TH QUEEN'S ROYAL LANCERS
JULY 3, 1879
BATTLE OF ULUNDI, ZULULAND

The third son of the Marquess of Waterford, the young Anglo-Irish aristocrat was educated at Eton, and then in Bonn, in what was then part of the Kingdom of Prussia. Aged 20, Beresford joined the 9th Queen's Royal Lancers as a cornet, the junior officer rank, and in 1876 was appointed aide-de-camp to the outgoing Viceroy of India, Thomas George Baring, 1st Earl Northbrook.

Beresford was kept on as military secretary by Northbrook's successor, Robert Bulwer-Lytton, 1st Earl of Lytton and in 1878 he was given permission to join his regiment for Lytton's greatest administrative folly - the 2nd Anglo-Afghan War - where he was mentioned in dispatches. He was again given leave to sail for Durban and join the general staff for the Anglo-Zulu War.

With Sergeant Edmund O'Toole of the Frontier Light Horse, Beresford defied an overwhelming Zulu charge at the Battle of Ulundi to recover Sergeant Fitzmaurice of the 24th Regiment of Foot who was pinned under his fallen horse. The valiant dash was witnessed by the war correspondent Archibald Forbes and recounted under the title "The Bravest Deed I Ever" saw, in which he wrote:

"The Zulus were perilously close to the poor fellow, but Beresford believed that

ABOVE · *A suitably gallant photograph of Lord Beresford wearing a full-dress tunic.*

LEFT · *Lord William Beresford riding to the rescue of the reconnaissance party on the eve of the Battle of Ulundi. How lucky for him that he managed to earn his VC with a journalist present.*

he saw a chance of anticipating them. Galloping back to the wounded man, and dismounting, he confronted his adversaries with his revolver, while urging the fallen soldier to get on [Bereford's] horse. The wounded man bade Beresford remount and fly... [Beresford] turned on the wounded man and swore with clenched fist that he would punch his head if he did not assist in the saving of his life. This droll argument prevailed. Still facing his foes with his revolver, Beresford partly lifted, partly hustled, the man into the saddle then, set his chestnut a-going after the other horsemen."

His VC was awarded on August 24, 1879 and according to Forbes, Beresford took the opportunity to tell the Queen that O'Toole "deserves infinitely greater credit than any that might attach to him."

Retiring after 33 years in uniform, Booth died December 8, 1899 and is buried in St Michael's Churchyard in his industrial hometown of Brierley Hill, Staffordshire. His medals are held by the Staffordshire Regiment Museum, Lichfield.

LIEUTENANT GONVILLE BROMHEAD
2/24TH REGIMENT OF FOOT
JANUARY 22-23, 1879
BATTLE OF RORKE'S DRIFT, NATAL COLONY

Despite his less than impressive military record (detailed on page 53), Bromhead came from a prestigious military pedigree. His father was Major Sir Edmund de Gonville Bromhead, 3rd Baronet who had served in the Battle of Waterloo (1815), his grandfather and namesake Sir Gonville Bromhead had fought in the American Revolutionary War (1775-1783), and his great-grandfather, Broadman Bromhead, had fought at the Battle of Quebec (1759).

Posted to Cape Colony for the closing stages of the 9th Frontier War, 'Gunny' was second-in-command of Rorke's Drift and commander of B Company, 2/24th Regiment of Foot for the battle. Following the clash, he became increasingly withdrawn

LEFT · *The fame of Chard and Bromhead began to grate on some of their peers. With musical tributes like this doing the rounds, it's easy to see why.*

ABOVE · *Lieutenant Gonville Bromhead before the Anglo-Zulu War, wearing an officer's forage cap (infantry and NCOs typically wore a shako) and the blue patrol jacket, like the one he would have worn at Rorke's Drift.*

Beresford returned to India and horse racing, and became the third husband of glamorous American socialite, Lillian Spencer-Churchill, Duchess of Marlborough. Eventually promoted to lieutenant colonel and awarded Knight Commander of the Order of the Indian Empire, Beresford passed away December 30, 1900 aged 53 from complications associated with the abdominal condition peritonitis.

Beresford is buried in the family vault in Clonagam Churchyard, Curraghmore, County Waterford, Ireland. His medals are privately owned.

SERGEANT ANTHONY CLARKE BOOTH
80TH REGIMENT OF FOOT
(STAFFORDSHIRE VOLUNTEERS)
MARCH 12, 1879
BATTLE OF INTOMBE, ZULULAND

Booth's steadfast rallying of the 80th Regiment when his commanding officer was slain, and the second-in-command bolted, is described in the article beginning on page 84.

The *London Gazette* reported his rank as colour sergeant at the time of the engagement, but he was actually promoted on March 13 to replace an NCO killed in action. Booth's VC was delayed by the looming court martial of Lieutenant Henry Harward for cowardice in the battle, and only once the trial had begun was the award confirmed. Booth received his VC on June 26, 1880.

Later he was appointed sergeant instructor of the 1st Volunteer Battalion of the South Staffordshire Regiment, which was created by the amalgamation of the 80th Regiment of Foot (Staffordshire Volunteers) with the 38th (1st Staffordshire) Regiment of Foot in 1881.

and lethargic, and Lord Chelmsford's recommendation of the VC (normally done by the recipient's direct superior, not his general) was seen by many of Bromhead's peers as a purely political gesture designed to overshadow the catastrophe at Isandlwana.

Major Francis Clery, who took command of Rorke's Drift after the battle and worked with Bromhead, mused: "Reputations are being made and lost here in an almost comical fashion... [Bromhead is a] capital fellow at everything except soldiering."

It was an assessment of his abilities that was echoed by Lieutenant Henry Curling, Royal Artillery, the only frontline British officer to survive the bloodshed of Isandlwana. He wrote: "Bromhead is a stupid old fellow, as deaf as a post. Is it not curious how some men are forced into notoriety?"

Lieutenant Colonel Redvers Buller around the time of Sudan Campaign as he was gazetted major general in 1884.

Lieutenant General Garnet Wolseley, VC, who replaced Lord Chelmsford as commander, was forced to present the men with their medals and privately regarded the whole business as a farce. He wrote scathingly in his journal: "I have now given away these decorations to both the officers who took part in the defence of Rorke's Drift and two duller, more stupid, more uninteresting men or less like gentlemen it has not been my luck to meet for a long time."

Promoted to captain and then major, Bromhead went with the 24th to fight in the 3rd Anglo-Burmese War (1885). It was in British India on February 9, 1892 that Bromhead died of typhoid fever aged 45 and is buried in the New Cantonment Cemetery in Allahabad, India. His medals are held by the Regimental Museum of the Royal Welsh in Brecon.

LIEUTENANT EDWARD STEVENSON BROWNE
1/24TH REGIMENT OF FOOT
MARCH 28, 1879
BATTLE OF KAMBULA, ZULULAND

As a member of the Mounted Infantry at the disastrous Battle of Hlobane, the 26-year old Browne twice raced back up the sheer track of Devil's Path to help his comrades escape the pursuing Zulu. He was awarded the VC on June 17, 1879 and presented with his medal by Wolseley on August 22, 1879.

Staying with the regiment for the rest of his career and being steadily promoted, Browne received his final rank of brigadier general in 1902 and retired in 1906. He died in Switzerland the following year at the age of 53 from chronic heart disease.

He was buried in an unmarked grave in Cimetiere de Clarens, Montreux - since repurposed - and his medals are held by the Regimental Museum of the Royal Welsh, Brecon.

LIEUTENANT COLONEL REDVERS HENRY BULLER
60TH (KING'S ROYAL RIFLE CORPS)
MARCH 28, 1879
BATTLE OF HLOBANE, ZULULAND

Born to an old Cornish family, Buller went to Eton and then joined the 60th (King's Royal Rifle Corps) where he served in the 2nd Opium War (1856-1860) and was promoted to captain ahead of the Red River Expedition (1870) to Canada. Attached to Wolseley's staff as intelligence officer in the Ashanti War in 1873, he was rewarded by a promotion to major and appointment as Companion of the Order of Bath. »

BELOW LEFT · *Buller's memorial tablet in Exeter Cathedral. He grew up in Devon and remained popular in the county despite his mauling in the press.* ANDREW R ABBOTT CC BY-SA 4.0

BELOW · *The statue of General Buller in Exeter was unveiled September 6, 1905 in tribute to the former commander in chief of the British forces in the Second Boer War.* PETER CLARKSON CC BY 2.0

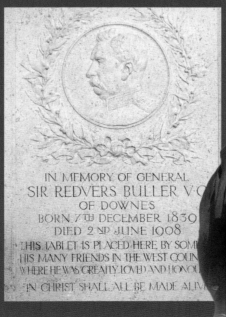

IN MEMORY OF GENERAL
SIR REDVERS BULLER V·C
OF DOWNES
BORN 7TH DECEMBER 1839
DIED 2ND JUNE 1908
THIS TABLET IS PLACED HERE BY SOME
HIS MANY FRIENDS IN THE WEST COUN
WHERE HE WAS GREATLY LOVED AND HONOU
IN CHRIST SHALL ALL BE MADE ALIVE

ABOVE · *Major Chard in 1881 wearing Royal Engineers full dress uniform, minus the helmet of course.*

RIGHT · *Lieutenant Chard's Victoria Cross and South Africa Medal, the latter awarded for service in the Anglo-Zulu War.* LORD ASHCROFT AND THE LORD ASHCROFT MEDAL COLLECTION

RIGHT · *Chard's memorial in Rochester Cathedral, Kent, which has an association with the Royal Engineers dating to the establishment of the Royal School of Military Engineering in nearby Chatham in 1812.*
HUGH LLEWELYN CC BY-SA 2.0

An aggressive and instinctive commander, Buller found his metier raising irregular units in the 9th Frontier War and continued in that vein into the Anglo-Zulu War, where he commanded the Frontier Light Horse. In a career filled with daring, his VC seemed almost low key as he raced back to rescue three men who had lost their horses during the chaotic retreat down the mountain at the Battle of Hlobane.

After serving in further colonial campaigns, Buller was promoted to general in 1896 and was appointed commander of the Natal Field Force in 1899, leading the British forces in the Second Boer War (1899-1902). Just as British defeat killed the career of his old friend Sir Evelyn Wood in the First Boer War some 19 years earlier, Buller's reputation never recovered from the ugly ambiguity and early defeats in South Africa. He was scapegoated by the government and dismissed.

Buller died June 2, 1908 aged 68 at the family home of Downes House, Crediton, Devon and is buried in the churchyard of Holy Cross. His Victoria Cross is held by the Royal Green Jackets (Rifles) Museum, Winchester.

LIEUTENANT JOHN ROUSE MERRIOTT CHARD
ROYAL ENGINEERS
JANUARY 22-23, 1879
BATTLE OF RORKE'S DRIFT, NATAL COLONY

As with Lieutenant Bromhead, Chard's VC was subject to some disbelief and the events that led to his award are described in detail in the article that begins on page 50.

The abrasive Wolseley made his feelings clear, writing in his journal: "A more uninteresting or more stupid looking fellow I never saw. [Colonel] Wood tells me he is a most useless officer, fit for nothing." In fact, Wolseley's disdain for Chard was so great that he presented him with his Victoria Cross in the field, rather than arranging a ceremony.

Much like Bromhead's battered reputation, it's impossible to discern just how much of the criticism was rooted in envy from their fellow officers or was a way of undermining the outgoing general, Lord Chelmsford. If the poisonous assessment of both men's capabilities is true, then that they were able to rally the defence of Rorke's Drift and hold out through the night is surely rendered even more heroic.

Chard met Queen Victoria twice at Balmoral and had been invited for a third meeting but was diagnosed with tongue cancer soon after, the dividend from a life of heavy smoking. He died at his brother's home in Somerset on November 1, 1897 at the age of 49.

Her Majesty, who was very fond of Chard, received regular reports on his condition. At his funeral, a wreath of laurel leaves was placed on the grave on behalf of the Queen, along with a note which read in her handwriting: "A mark of admiration and regard for a brave soldier from his Sovereign, Victoria."

Chard is buried in St John the Baptist churchyard, Hatch Beauchamp, Somerset. His medals were acquired by the actor Stanley Baker, who played Chard in the film *Zulu*, although the VC was listed as a replica and the set was picked up at a bargain price. Later authenticated, the medals were purchased by the Ashcroft Trust and can be seen in the Lord Ashcroft Gallery at the Imperial War Museum, London.

LIEUTENANT NEVILL JOSIAH AYLMER COGHILL
1/24TH REGIMENT OF FOOT
22 JANUARY 1879
BATTLE OF ISANDLWANA, ZULULAND

A charming 25-year old Irish officer, whose knee injury incurred during a foraging party

General Wolseley presents Chard with his Victoria Cross in the field. He was so incensed by the VCs his predecessor had sanctioned that he wanted to avoid any ceremony.

Lieutenant Nevill Coghill in civilian clothes prior to the outbreak of the Anglo-Zulu War.

to the assistance of his friend, though at the time he was wholly incapacitated from walking, and but too well aware that any accident that might separate him from his horse must be fatal to him."

At the time of Coghill and Melvill's deaths, the Victoria Cross was not awarded posthumously but 30 years later the mood had changed. Coghill's VC was presented to his younger brother, Sir Egerton Coghill, 5th Baronet in 1907, the result of years of campaigning by the boys' late father, Sir John Joscelyn Coghill, 4th Baronet.

Coghill is buried at Fugitives' Drift, near to where he fell. Several trophies collected by him in Africa are held by the National Museum of Ireland, Dublin and his medals can be viewed at the Regimental Museum of the Royal Welsh, Brecon.

ACTING ASSISTANT COMMISSARY JAMES LANGLEY DALTON
COMMISSARIAT AND TRANSPORT DEPARTMENT
JANUARY 22-23, 1879
BATTLE OF RORKE'S DRIFT, NATAL COLONY

The role of the veteran NCO at Rorke's Drift can be found on page 53, but curiously his influence on the outcome of the action was slow to be recognised. Some historians suggested this may have been for class reasons, as Dalton was a Londoner of Irish Catholic stock and raised

LEFT · *Acting Assistant Commissary James Dalton, arguably the officer who did the most to save Rorke's Drift.*

from the ranks, but that is to ignore the seven private soldiers and corporals awarded the Victoria Cross in the same action.

A better explanation is that Dalton's military status was ambiguous at the time. Although he had 22 years' service under his belt, he had retired in 1871 and was technically a civilian. Furthermore, as he had relocated to southern Africa, he may have been considered a colonial. It's possible Chelmsford didn't really believe Dalton qualified.

Following the cessation of hostilities, the 2/24th Regiment of Foot were marching through Pietermaritzburg, Natal, when one of them spotted Dalton and pulled the

a few days earlier left him in no position to fight on foot, Coghill was unable to even mount his horse without help and so retreat from the massacre at Isandlwana is doubly understandable. Controversy surrounds the extent to which his riding partner Lieutenant Melvill, cradling the Queen's colours, had been trying to recast his own flight as an act of heroism (see page 46).

Regardless of Melvill's motives, Coghill died trying to save his comrade as he was swept down the Buffalo River. In a report to Lord Chelmsford, Colonel Richard Glyn, the commander of No.3 Column, explained: "His horse had carried him safely across, but on looking round for Lieutenant Melvill and seeing him struggling to save the colour in the river, he at once turned his horse and rode back into the stream again to Lieutenant Melvill's assistance.

"It would appear that now the enemy had assembled in considerable force along their own bank, and had opened a heavy fire on our people, directing it more especially on Lieutenant Melvill, who wore a red patrol jacket. So that when Lieutenant Coghill got into the river again, his horse was almost immediately killed by a bullet. Lieutenant Coghill was thus cast loose in the stream also."

Their bodies were found by the riverbank two weeks later, surrounded by Zulu dead and the sunken Queen's colours were recovered from the riverbed.

Glyn concluded: "I would draw His Excellency's attention to the equally noble and gallant conduct of Lieutenant Coghill, who did not hesitate for an instant to return, unsolicited, and ride again into the river, under a heavy fire of the enemy,

46-year old veteran over, exclaiming: "Why there's Mr Dalton cheering us! We ought to be cheering him! He was the best man there!"

Thanks to petitioning from other officers and a campaign in the press, Dalton was presented with his Victoria Cross by Major General Hugh Clifford, VC at a parade on January 16, 1880.

Returning to England soon after, Dalton was lured back to Africa by the 1886 Witwatersrand Gold Rush in Transvaal and acquired shares in a mine. While staying with an old army friend in Port Elizabeth, Cape Colony, he died in his sleep on January 8, 1887. Dalton is buried at Russell Road Roman Catholic cemetery, Port Elizabeth, South Africa, and his Victoria Cross is held at the Royal Logistic Corps Museum, Camberley, Surrey.

CAPTAIN HENRY CECIL DUDGEON D'ARCY

FRONTIER LIGHT HORSE
JULY 3, 1879
BATTLE OF ULUNDI, ZULULAND
The first New Zealand-born Victoria Cross recipient, D'Arcy was a thoroughbred colonial adventurer in the spirit of his father. Major Oliver D'Arcy had been posted first to New Zealand with 65th (2nd Yorkshire, North Riding) Regiment of Foot, then to Cape Colony with the 18th (The Royal Irish) Regiment of Foot, and finally transferred into the locally raised Cape Mounted Riflemen, with a view to retiring in Africa.

Briefly working as a clerk, Henry D'Arcy followed his father into the irregular cavalry, joining the Albany Mounted Volunteers in 1877 where he was soon promoted to lieutenant. A few months later he switched to the Frontier Light Horse and in April 1878 came under the command of the energetic Lieutenant Colonel Buller.

D'Arcy was first put forward for the Victoria Cross for his role in the Battle of Kambula, where during the frantic flight down Devil's Pass, he gave his horse to a wounded trooper and then fought on foot for the rest of the descent. This was turned down as D'Arcy was a colonial volunteer and not a member of the regular British Army (this sort of inconsistency can perhaps explain the attitude to James Langley Dalton earlier).

He tried to repeat the feat at the Battle of Ulundi. Now captain and in command of the Frontier Light Horse, D'Arcy rode out to rescue a trooper who had fallen from his horse but the two men being too

heavy, D'Arcy's mount threw them both. The trooper was captured by the Zulu and tortured long into the night, while D'Arcy escaped by the skin of his teeth having tried and failed to get the wounded man back onto his saddle.

For this, D'Arcy finally received the Victoria Cross, which was presented by Wolseley in Pretoria, Transvaal on December 10, 1879. It was a change of mood to appease the grumbling colonial authorities, who had endured a war in their back garden and sent their sons to fight but were receiving little recognition. In his speech, Wolseley said: "It will now be understood, from the gift of this decoration by Her Majesty, that Her Majesty does not reserve

this honour for imperial troops alone but is anxious to distinguish the courage and devotion of the soldiers of her colonial empire."

Wolseley being Wolseley, recorded in his journal: "I don't think he was a good case for the citation, as he did not succeed in saving the life of the man he dismounted to assist."

The Frontier Light Horse was disbanded after the war. D'Arcy joined the revived Cape Mounted Riflemen for more reckless glory but was forced to resign his commission amid rumours of drunkenness and depression. Suffering from malaria and the tropical disease, bilharzia (schistosomiasis), D'Arcy needed a break and in August 1881 went to stay with friends of his parents at a remote mission station.

D'Arcy vanished during the night. Three months later a body was discovered in a cave in Amatola Forest, six miles from the mission. As it was wearing D'Arcy's clothes, it

PRIVATE FREDERICK HITCH V.C. 1856~1913 Hero of Rorke's Drift lived and died here

ABOVE · Private Frederick Hitch with one arm in a discreet leather sling. This photograph may have been taken directly before he was awarded his Victoria Cross as there are other images from the same time with him wearing it.

was assumed he had wandered off, perhaps to kill himself, and died of exposure. He was given a full military funeral and laid to rest in King William's Town Cemetery, South Africa. His Victoria Cross is in private ownership.

Decades later someone came forward claiming to have spoken to D'Arcy at a cricket match in 1925. He said he had been sworn to secrecy, that the troubled hero explained he had found a dead man in the forest. Seeing an opportunity to change his fortunes, D'Arcy traded clothes with the unlucky forester and vanished to Natal to live under an assumed name.

PRIVATE EDMUND JOHN FOWLER
90TH REGIMENT OF FOOT (PERTHSHIRE VOLUNTEERS)
MARCH 28, 1879
BATTLE OF HLOBANE, ZULULAND

The 18-year old Fowler found himself attached to Wood's escort with the Mounted Infantry and followed Captain the Honourable Ronald Campbell and Lieutenant Henry Lysons to clear a cave of Zulu marksmen (described on page 66). Colonel Wood marvelled that their daring dash through the rocks was "the greatest deed I ever saw performed in my life."

Fowler's Victoria Cross came via the obstinate father of Lieutenant Lysons, General Sir Daniel Lysons, who spent three years lobbying the army and pulling strings until his son was finally presented the VC, and Fowler was carried along with him, on April 13, 1882.

He very nearly lost it. Court martialled later that year for embezzling money, he was sentenced to surrender his medals. However, Queen Victoria intervened, and his medals were restored. Following a medical discharge in 1900, Fowler opened a pub, the Live and Let Live, in Colchester and the next year was in court for serving beer after hours. He turned up with his medals on full display and his citation was read aloud, leading to his acquittal by the garrison town's suitably patriotic jury.

Fowler sold his VC at auction in 1906 and passed away March 26, 1926 at his home in Colchester aged 64. His last years may have been inglorious, but he was laid to rest with all due reverence - his coffin was carried on a gun carriage, while a piper from the Cameronians (Scottish Rifles), the successor of the 90th Regiment, played The Flowers of the Forest.

Fowler is buried at Colchester Cemetery, Essex and his Victoria Cross is displayed at the Cameronians Regimental Museum in the Hamilton Low Parks Museum, Hamilton.

PRIVATE FREDERICK HITCH
2/24TH REGIMENT OF FOOT
JANUARY 22-23, 1879
BATTLE OF RORKE'S DRIFT, NATAL COLONY

With Corporal Allen, the 22-year old Hitch covered the field hospital at Rorke's Drift (detailed on page 56) and was also incapacitated after being shot in the shoulder. Hitch's wound was far more serious, and the bone completely shattered.

He was invalided back to Britain and was convalescing at the Royal Victoria Military Hospital in Netley, Hampshire when he was presented with his VC.

Due to the difficulty in using his right arm, Hitch struggled to find steady work and was forced to provide for his eight living children on a meagre disability pension. Even when he did find employment, he was beset by misfortune. Falling from a ladder, he awoke in hospital to discover his Victoria Cross - which he always wore - was missing.

The army forced him to pay for a replacement and he lost his job when he was accused of faking the accident to cover for having sold his medal, although there was no proof he had done so. He then found some success with a horse-drawn and then motor taxi company. When he collapsed and died in January 6, 1913, aged 56, his funeral was attended by admiring London cabbies.

He is buried at St Nicholas Churchyard, Chiswick and he is remembered by the Hitch Award for Bravery, which is presented by the Worshipful Company of Hackney Carriage Drivers. His VC is held by the Regimental Museum of the Royal Welsh, Brecon.

PRIVATE ALFRED HENRY 'HARRY' HOOK
2/24TH REGIMENT OF FOOT
JANUARY 22-23, 1879
BATTLE OF RORKE'S DRIFT, NATAL COLONY

The role of the 28-year old Gloucestershire native in evacuating the patients from the field hospital at Rorke's Drift is described in detail on page 57, as well as the differences between the real Hook and his unsavoury counterpart depicted in the film *Zulu*. Alone of the defenders, Hook's VC was presented at the site of the battle itself - a fact he remained justifiably proud of throughout his life.

Discharged in June 1880, Hook returned to Britain to discover that his wife had remarried, hearing that he had been killed in action. Although he struggled to find work, he maintained his links to the uniform by serving as a sergeant-instructor in 1st Volunteer Battalion, Royal Fusiliers in London.

Eventually, Lord Chelmsford, Bromhead, and even the Prince of Wales intervened to find him a job at the British Museum. Starting out as an inside duster, he was then appointed attendant to the Reading Room. Resigning due to ill health and returning to Gloucester, he died aged 54 of pulmonary tuberculosis on March 12, 1905.

He is buried at St Andrew's Churchyard, Churcham, Gloucestershire and his Victoria

Cross is on display at the Regimental Museum of the Royal Welsh, Brecon.

PRIVATE ROBERT JONES
2/24TH REGIMENT OF FOOT
JANUARY 22-23, 1879
BATTLE OF RORKE'S DRIFT, NATAL COLONY

The 21-year old Welshman, along with his English compatriot Private William Jones, earned their award for their gallant defence of the hospital, as detailed on page 57.

Despite being stabbed four times, burned, and shot in the battle, Jones returned to active service with the 24th in Gibraltar and India. After returning to Britain and spending time in the army reserve, he finally surrendered his red tunic in 1888. He found work as an agricultural labourer in the employ of Major de la Hay in Peterchurch, Herefordshire, but was unable to adjust to civilian life.

Jones was tormented by the uneasy

ABOVE · *An engraving of Alfred Henry Hook with the rank of sergeant in the 1st Volunteer Battalion, Royal Fusiliers.*

memories of Rorke's Drift. He was drinking heavily, and his family reported that he suffered from recurring nightmares. On September 6, 1898, he borrowed a shotgun from de la Hay to - he claimed - scare away crows. A single shot was heard, and Jones was found dead, aged 41. The shell had entered through his mouth.

A verdict of 'suicide while insane' was given by the coroner. Jones is buried at St Peter's Churchyard, Peterchurch - his headstone facing away from the church as suicide was taboo - and his Victoria Cross is on display in the Lord Ashcroft Gallery at the Imperial War Museum, London.

PRIVATE WILLIAM JONES
2/24TH REGIMENT OF FOOT
JANUARY 22-23, 1879
BATTLE OF RORKE'S DRIFT, NATAL
COLONY

Though older than Robert Jones - William Jones was 39 at the time of Rorke's Drift - his age was no shield against the long-term damage done by the brutal close-quarter fight in the burning hospital.

Above · Private William Jones holds the Zulu back with his bayonet while his comrades get the wounded to safety. They were unlikely to be sitting around in nightshirts during a battle.

Right · Jones's grave in Philips Park Cemetery, Manchester. He was originally buried in a pauper's plot and the headstone was paid for by public subscription. PLUCAS58 CC BY-SA 4.0

Three weeks after the battle, Jones was discharged on health grounds due to his chronic rheumatism which he attributed to sleeping on the cold, wet ground during the Anglo-Zulu War. His hands ruined by the desperate tunnelling through the hospital walls, Jones monetised his heroism instead. He gave public talks on the battle and toured as part of Buffalo Bill's Wild West Show, restaging the Battle of Rorke's Drift for the braying punters.

When interest dried up in 1910, he was forced to pawn his Victoria Cross to make ends meet and a year later, Jones was found wandering the streets of Manchester in a state of confusion.

The police reunited him with his family and his last two years were spent at his daughter's home until his mental state deteriorated further and he became convinced the Zulu were coming in through the windows. He grabbed his grandchildren and fled. Institutionalised, he died soon afterwards on April 15, 1913, aged 73 and was given a pauper's grave.

Jones is buried in Philips Park Cemetery, Manchester. His VC is on display at the Regimental Museum of The Royal Welsh, Brecon.

MAJOR WILLIAM KNOX-LEET
1/13TH (1ST SOMERSETSHIRE) (PRINCE ALBERT'S LIGHT INFANTRY) REGIMENT OF FOOT
MARCH 28, 1879
BATTLE OF HLOBANE, ZULULAND

Above · Knox-Leet as commander of the 2nd Battalion Prince Albert's (Somerset Light Infantry) in Burma.

The son of an Anglican vicar in Dalkey, Ireland, Knox-Leet studied at Trinity College and joined the 13th (1st Somersetshire) (Prince Albert's Light Infantry) Regiment of Foot as an ensign. Narrowly missing out on the Crimean War, Lieutenant Knox-Leet joined the reinforcements mobilised to suppress the Indian Mutiny. He was mentioned in dispatches for his role in the actions at Amora and Nugger in April 1858.

After a series of staff roles that saw him advance to major, Knox-Leet joined the 13th Regiment in the Cape Colony and was put in charge of Wood's Irregulars, two auxiliary battalions of Africans hostile to the Zulu King. Hurting his knee during a game of tug-o-war between the officers of the 13th and 90th Regiments, Colonel Wood ordered Knox-Leet to sit out the Battle of Hlobane, but he refused.

As with many of the VCs awarded in that disastrous action, Knox-Leet rescued Lieutenant Metcalfe Smith of the Frontier Light Horse, whose mount had been shot out from under him. Knox-Leet especially couldn't afford to be

*TO THE MEMORY OF
PRIVATE 593
WILLIAM JONES V.C.
B. COY. 2/24th REGT. OF FOOT.
AWARDED THE VICTORIA CROSS
FOR GALLANTRY AT THE DEFENCE
OF THE MISSION AT RORKES DRIFT,
NATAL PROVINCE, SOUTH AFRICA
22nd/23rd JANUARY 1879.
DIED MANCHESTER 15th APRIL 1913.
AGED 73 YEARS.*

IN MEMORY OF

caught on foot either with his knee injury. His own horse had been shot, so he saddled up a pack mule, and then when that was shot, he mounted another horse, this one roaming without a bridle.

With one of the officers of Wood's Irregulars giving his own life to cover Knox-Leet and Smith's descent down the rough track of Devil's Pass, both men made it to safety. Despite his ordeal, Knox-Leet was back in action the next day, leading two companies of irregulars at the Battle of Kambula for which he was mentioned in dispatches.

ABOVE · *Lysons in the doublet of a captain of the Cameronians (Scottish Rifles). He wears the Egyptian Khedive's Star for service in the Sudan Campaign of 1884-1886, as well as service medals for Sudan and southern Africa, and his VC.*

Eventually promoted to lieutenant colonel and then colonel commanding 2/13th Regiment, he led the battalion in the Third Anglo-Burmese War (1885–87), earning a further mention in dispatches.

Retiring with the rank of major general, Knox-Leet passed away at Great Chart, Kent

LEFT · *Knox-Leet's grave in Great Chart, Kent.*

on June 29, 1898, aged 65. He is buried in St Mary the Virgin Churchyard, Great Chart and his Victoria Cross is held by the Somerset Light Infantry Museum, Taunton.

LIEUTENANT HENRY LYSONS
2/90TH REGIMENT OF FOOT (PERTHSHIRE VOLUNTEERS)
MARCH 28, 1879
BATTLE OF HLOBANE, ZULULAND
As Colonel Wood's aide-de-camp, the 20-year-old Lysons joined Captain Campbell and Private Fowler in clearing the cave of snipers at the Battle of Hlobane.

As explored in Fowler's entry, a Victoria Cross for such a minor action in comparison to others in the campaign came courtesy Lysons' pushy father, who applied a good deal of pressure. General Sir Daniel Lysons, a distinguished Crimean War veteran and Quartermaster General of the British Army, felt very strongly that his son had earned a VC and it was difficult for a mere colonel to disagree. General Lysons wasn't the only proud parent who attempted to leverage his own position on behalf of his offspring, but he was the only one with the high enough rank to succeed.

Present for the Battle of Kambula and the Battle of Ulundi where he was mentioned in dispatches, Lysons was serving in ≫

Lieutenant Lysons is shown recovering the sword of the Prince Imperial and presenting it to Lord Chelmsford, unfortunately, this event seems only to exist in the imagination of the Illustrated London News.

India when his Victoria Cross was issued, and it was presented by Colonel Craig at Cawnpore on August 18, 1882.

Later promoted to colonel and appointed Commander of the Order of Bath, Lysons died suddenly aged 49 on July 24, 1907. He is buried in St Peter's Churchyard, Rodmarton,

RIGHT · *Lieutenant Teignmouth Melvill in civilian clothes prior to the Anglo-Zulu War.*

Gloucestershire and his medals are held by the Cameronians (Scottish Rifles) Regimental Museum, Hamilton.

LIEUTENANT TEIGNMOUTH MELVILL

24TH REGIMENT OF FOOT

JANUARY 22, 1879

BATTLE OF ISANDLWANA, ZULULAND

The son of the Military Secretary of the East India Company, Melvill was educated at Harrow and Cambridge before joining 1/24th where he served as unremarkable adjutant until disaster at Isandlwana brought him to notice.

As explained on page 46, there is some controversy surrounding Melvill's actions and there's no primary source for the order to save the colours, simply a rumour conjured up in the mess hall by defeated men searching for some glimmer of valour.

The attempt to save the colours has become part of the lore of the Anglo-Zulu War and makes for a thrilling climax to 1979 film *Zulu Dawn*. It was just the tonic the British public needed after Isandlwana - if British soldiers had to die, it was better they died boldly doing their duty. Queen Victoria was so moved by the story that she had the *London Gazette* issue a notice saying that had both Coghill and Melvill survived, they would have been awarded the Victoria Cross.

Even Chelmsford was dubious about whether Melvill deserved the VC, writing: "His ride was not more daring than that of those who escaped. The question, therefore, remains had he succeeded in saving the colours and his own life, would he have been considered to deserve the Victoria Cross?"

Wolseley, as ever, was uncompromising. He wrote in his journal: "I am sorry that both of these officers were not killed with their men at Isandlwana instead of where they were [...] It is monstrous making heroes of those who saved or attempted to save their lives by bolting."

Melvill is buried alongside Coghill at Fugitives' Drift, South Africa and his Victoria Cross is held by the Regimental Museum of The Royal Welsh, Brecon.

ABOVE · *Surgeon James Reynolds, often reported as a surgeon-major because his promotion was retroactively dated when it appeared in the London Gazette.*

SERGEANT EDMUND JOSEPH 'PADDY' O'TOOLE

FRONTIER LIGHT HORSE

3 JULY 1879

BATTLE OF ULUNDI, ZULULAND

Almost every part of Sergeant O'Toole's life outside of the Anglo-Zulu War is a mystery. What we know for certain is that he was born in Bray, County Wicklow, Ireland, and by 1879 he was a sergeant in the Frontier Light Horse.

At the Battle of Ulundi, O'Toole galloped out with Captain Beresford to rescue Sergeant Fitzmaurice of the 24th Regiment of Foot. It was opined by some of Beresford's contemporaries that he had joined the campaign with the express purpose of bagging himself a Victoria Cross, but he was certainly gracious enough to share his laurels with O'Toole.

Archibald Forbes, the war correspondent who documented the rescue, described Beresford hauling Fitzmaurice into his saddle and facing certain death until the Irish irregular intervened:

"A comrade, the brave Sergeant O'Toole, fortunately came back, shot down Zulu after Zulu with cool courage, and then aided Beresford in keeping the wounded man in the saddle until the laager was reached."

His VC was presented on January 16, 1880 in Pietermaritzburg by Major General Sir Henry Hugh Clifford. O'Toole later rose to the rank of captain and died 1891 in Salisbury, Rhodesia (now Harare, Zimbabwe), possibly having journeyed there with a pioneer column of the British South Africa Company. His resting place and the location of his medals are unknown.

SURGEON JAMES HENRY REYNOLDS

ARMY MEDICAL DEPARTMENT

JANUARY 22-23, 1879

BATTLE OF RORKE'S DRIFT, NATAL COLONY

Born in Dublin, Reynolds obtained his Bachelor of Medicine and Bachelor of Surgery at Trinity College in 1867 and joined the Army Medical Department in March the following year. He was stationed in India with the 36th (Herefordshire) Regiment of Foot from 1869 to 1870 but was invalided home when he found himself on the wrong side of the bedsheets in a cholera outbreak.

Posted to Cape Colony in August 1874, Reynolds joined the line infantry for the series of small frontier clashes that led up to the Anglo-Zulu War before he found himself commanding the field hospital at the mission station turned column depot of Rorke's Drift.

During the battle, Reynolds repeatedly raced out into the line of fire to treat the wounded and haul them into cover, as well as ferrying ammunition between the store and the field hospital. He was accompanied by his terrier, Dick, who was given an honourable mention in Reynolds' citation.

Reynolds remained at Rorke's Drift for several weeks to support the wounded and was promoted to surgeon-major (dated to January 23). He received his VC from Colonel Richard Glyn during a special parade of the 1/24th Regiment at Durban on August 26, 1879. The British Medical Association also honoured him with the Gold Medal.

There was some grumbling from the Army Medical Department that Bromhead and Chard had both been invited to the palace (Bromhead didn't get the message as he was on a fishing trip, but Chard got on famously with Her Majesty) and Reynolds had been overlooked. Although medical officers couldn't command frontline troops, a surgeon was entitled to the 'advantages' of his equivalent rank of lieutenant or captain.

Reynolds retired with the rank of brigade surgeon lieutenant colonel in 1896. He died on March 5, 1932 at the grand old age of 88, at which time he was the oldest living VC, both in terms of his age and the age of his award. Reynolds is buried in St Mary's Roman Catholic Cemetery, London and his Victoria Cross is displayed at the Army Medical Services Museum, Aldershot.

CORPORAL CHRISTIAN FERDINAND SCHIESS
2/3RD NATAL NATIVE CONTINGENT
JANUARY 22-23, 1879
BATTLE OF RORKE'S DRIFT, NATAL COLONY

The actions of Schiess, who set about the Zulu with great ferocity despite his wound, are detailed in depth on page 56. Only 22-years-old at the time of the Battle of Rorke's Drift, the Swiss national had been in uniform since the age of 15 and was perhaps the only man, save the aging Crimea veterans, to have fought against a modern European army, as he did in the Franco-Prussian War (1870-1871).

Schiess arrived in Cape Colony as part of an assisted passage scheme to attract Swiss labourers, but his real trade was the rifle and he enlisted in a volunteer company for the 9th Frontier War. He volunteered again

BELOW · *The British troop carrier HMS Serapis, on which the penniless Corporal Schiess was given passage to Britain. Ominously, named for a Greek god of the underworld, Schiess died during the voyage and was buried at sea.*

ABOVE · *Private Samuel Wassall in the uniform of the 80th Regiment of Foot (Staffordshire Volunteers). The collar facings were yellow.*

for the Anglo-Zulu War and while the white NCOs of the Natal Native Contingent often left much to be desired, Schiess was an experienced and dedicated soldier.

Awarded his VC at Pietermaritzburg on February 2, 1880 by Wolseley, Schiess was the first colonial of the Anglo-Zulu War to receive it and is still the only Swiss national in that

celebrated band of brothers.

Despite his valour, Schiess struggled to find work and even reached out to the British government for assistance, to no avail. Four years after Rorke's Drift he was living on the street in Cape Town, weak and emaciated from exposure and malnutrition. The Royal Navy offered him free passage to Britain to start a new life, but his health deteriorated further, and he died aboard HMS Serapis aged 28 on December 14, 1884.

Buried at sea off the coast of Angola, his Victoria Cross finished the voyage that its owner couldn't, and it is now held by the National Army Museum, London.

PRIVATE SAMUEL WASSALL
80TH REGIMENT OF FOOT (STAFFORDSHIRE VOLUNTEERS)
JANUARY 22, 1879
BATTLE OF ISANDLWANA, ZULULAND

Birmingham-born Wassall was 22 years old and serving with the Mounted Infantry when he broke out of the Zulu cordon around the camp and made it to the Buffalo River. He told his own story of the rescue of Private Westwood:

"I knew how dangerous the river was, there was a current running six or seven mile an hour, no ordinary man could swim it... I drove my horse into the torrent, thankful even to be in that »

Not knowing who either of the soldiers were and not witnessing the outcome of the rescue, Barton reported seeing two men drowned. Days later when visiting a comrade in the field hospital at Helpmekaar, Barton was describing the scene he had witnessed when a man in the ward piped up. Incredibly he had been overheard by Westwood. Barton and Westwood's accounts ensured that Wassall was awarded the Victoria Cross.

Wassall spent his final years in Cumbria and died in hospital in Barrow-in-Furness at the age of 70. He is buried in Barrow Cemetery and his medals are held by Staffordshire Regimental Museum, Lichfield.

PRIVATE JOHN WILLIAMS
2/24TH REGIMENT OF FOOT
JANUARY 22-23, 1879
BATTLE OF RORKE'S DRIFT, NATAL COLONY

Another of the men to defend the field hospital at Rorke's Drift, Williams held the Zulu at bay for three hours until his ammunition ran out

and with Private Hook began tunnelling through the internal walls to help the patients to safety.

His real name was John Fielding, and it's not known why the Welshman enlisted under a false identity. Whoever he might have been scarcely mattered to the men whose lives he saved, and Williams was presented with his Victoria Cross in Gibraltar on March 1, 1880 by Major General Anderson.

Going on to serve as sergeant in the 3rd Volunteer Battalion, South Wales Borderers, when the First World War broke out the 57-year old veteran volunteered once more and joined the civilian staff of the South Wales Borderers depot.

Williams died of heart failure at his daughter's home at Tycoch, Monmouthshire, on November 25, 1932, aged 75. He is buried in St Michael's Churchyard, Llantarnam and his medals are held at the Regimental Museum of The Royal Welsh, Brecon. Living on into the age of cinema, his funeral is preserved in a Pathé newsreel entitled 'Britain's Oldest VC' and available to view online. ◖◖◖◖

ABOVE · *Private John Williams, aka John Fielding. The Sphinx badge of the 24th Regiment of Foot is clearly visible on his collar.*

BELOW · *The medal group of Private Robert Jones. The "1877-8-9" on the clasp of his South Africa Medal reflect the fact that Jones had been present in Cape Colony for the small-scale frontier conflicts prior to the Anglo-Zulu War.* LORD ASHCROFT AND THE LORD ASHCROFT MEDAL COLLECTION

part and was urging him to the other side, when I heard a cry for help and I saw a man of my own regiment, a private named Westwood was being carried away. He was struggling, desperately and was drowning. The Zulus were sweeping down to the riverbank, which I had just left and there was a terrible temptation to go ahead and just save one's self, but I turned my horse around on the Zulu bank, got him there, dismounted, tied him up to a tree and I never tied him more swiftly.

"Then I struggled out to Westwood, got hold of him and struggled back to the horse with him. I scrambled up into the saddle, pulled Westwood after me and plunged into the torrent again, and as I did so the Zulus rushed up to the bank and let drive with their firearms and spears, but most mercifully I escaped them all and with a thankful heart urged my gallant horse up the steep bank on the Natal side and then got him to go as hard as he could towards Helpmekaar."

Unnoticed by either man, the rescue was watched by Captain William Barton of the Natal Native Horse and he marvelled: "I consider this man performed a most gallant and courageous act, in trying to save his comrade at almost certain risk of his own life."